Colophon

Title:	Service Agreements - A Management Guide
A publication of:	itSMF-NL
Lead Authors:	Robert Benyon and Robert Johnston
Editors:	Jan van Bon (chief editor)
	Arjen de Jong (editor)
Uitgever:	Van Haren Publishing, Zaltbommel-NL, www.vanharen.net
ISBN(10):	90 77212 91 4
ISBN(13):	978 90 77212 91 2
Edition:	First edition, first impression, September 2006

Design & Layout: CO2 Premedia, Amersfoort-NL

Printer: Wilco, Amersfoort-NL

For any further enquiries about Van Haren Publishing, please send an e-mail to:
info@vanharen.net

D1493090

Foreword

Ever seen an organization quarrel with their service provider? Me too, several times. And just as often I've seen these parties grabbing the same SLA to justify both their arguments. None of them understood why their business relationship ended up in a situation where they quarrel like competing politicians.

If you are looking at this Management Guide to get a nice template for an SLA then my advice would be that you are better off searching the Internet for it. The key message from this book is that it takes much more than a nice SLA to be successful in Service Management.

These days an IT manager does a bad job if he isn't able to demonstrate the quality of the services his organization is delivering. This isn't limited to having an SLA based on a nice template; equally important are the following: the whole structure of managing different services, reporting on services, managing expectations, complying with company or branch related standards, and having a framework to implement Service Management and setting up a Service Catalogue.

For the IT managers that are determined to accomplish the optimal relationship with customers and service providers this Management Guide could prove to be very valuable.

Arjen Droog
CEO itSMF Netherlands

Acknowledgments

This book is the result of the Masters research conducted by Robert Benyon and Robert Johnston. The research was undertaken in the Distributed Multimedia Centre of Excellence at Rhodes University, South Africa, with financial support from Telkom, Business Connexion, Converse, Verso Technologies, THRIP and the National Research Foundation. The author's respective theses explored Service Management and Service Agreements.

The authors would like to extend their appreciation and gratitude to their supervisor, Professor David Sewry. The extent of his support and dedication is only surpassed by his meticulous attention to detail. For his encouragement, ideas, comments and criticisms we are most grateful.

The authors would also like to acknowledge the support and encouragement from their respective families who have made studying at Rhodes University possible.

A very important role was played by the review team. This team was composed of a wide variety of professionals from various countries:

- Ton Alofs - Steenbok Adviesgroep, Netherlands
- Peter Blom - Synergie in Uitvoering BV, Netherlands
- Oskar Brink - Shell Information Technology International, Malaysia
- Peter H.M. Brooks - Phmb Consulting, South Africa
- Jurian Burgers - Simac ICT Nederland, Netherlands
- Matthew Burrows – BSMimpact.com, United Kingdom
- David Clifford - Pro Attivo, United Kingdom
- Federico Corradi – Cogitek, Italy
- Marc Drost - Océ-Technologies BV, Netherlands
- Bart den Dulk – Port of Rotterdam, Netherlands
- John Groom - West-Groom Consulting, United Kingdom
- David Jones - Plan-Net, United Kingdom
- Peter de Koning - De Lage Landen, Netherlands
- Marcel van de Laarschot - Defensie Telematica Organisatie, Netherlands
- Adrian Leach – Putteridge Consulting / Parity, United Kingdom
- Hikmet Ozermis – INQA, Netherlands
- Rian de Putter - Verdonck, Klooster & Associates, Netherlands
- Dean Taylor - VEGA Group PLC, United Kingdom
- Wilbert Teunissen – Sogeti, Netherlands
- Peter Jan Teuns – Meerschap, Netherlands

- Nico de Vos - Rendeck Automatisering BV, Netherlands
- Anouk Vromans – CZ Actief in Gezondheid, Netherlands
- Rob van der Waal – Nerefco B.V., Netherlands
- Wilfred Wah – PA Consulting Group, Hong Kong
- Gert Zondervan – Maintain, Netherlands

Together, they raised a good twelve hundred issues that were all taken into account by the editor and the authors team. In this way, we hope we have achieved best practice in the truest sense of the word, having lots of experts contributing their 'private best practice' experiences, and merging these into a consistent whole.

The overall editorial process was led by Jan van Bon, itSMF-NL's chief editor. He guided the book through the thorough and formal endorsement procedure by itSMF's International Publication Executive Sub-Committee (IPESC), resulting in confirmation that this publication was to be considered 'global best practice', supported by the international itSMF community.

Given the desire for a broad consensus in the IT Service Management field, new developments, additional material and other contributions from IT Service Management professionals are welcomed to extend and further improve this publication. Any forwarded material will be discussed by the editorial team and where appropriate incorporated into new editions. Any comments can be sent to the chief editor, email: jan.van.bon@itsmf.nl.

Service Agreements - A Management Guide

About the ITSM Library

The publications in the ITSM Library cover best practice in IT Management and are published on behalf of itSMF Netherlands (itSMF-NL).

The IT Service Management Forum (itSMF) is the association for IT service organizations, and for customers of IT services. itSMF's goal is to promote innovation and support of IT management; suppliers and customers are equally represented within the itSMF. The Forum's main focus is exchange of peer knowledge and experience. Our authors are global experts.

The following publications are, or soon will be, available.

Introduction, Foundations and Practitioners books
- Foundations of IT Service Management based on ITIL® / IT Service Management – an introduction, based on ITIL® (Arabic, Danish, German, English, French, Italian, Japanese, Korean, Dutch, Brazilian Portuguese, Russian, and Spanish)
- IT Services Procurement – an introduction based on ISPL (Dutch)
- Project Management based on Prince2 (Dutch, English, German)
- Practitioner Release & Control for IT Service Management, based on ITIL (English)

IT Service Management – best practices
- IT Service Management – best practices, part 1 (Dutch)
- IT Service Management – best practices, part 2 (Dutch)
- IT Service Management – best practices, part 3 (Dutch)

Topics & Management instruments
- Metrics for IT Service Management (English)
- Six Sigma for IT Management (English)
- The RfP for IT Outsourcing (Dutch)
- Service Agreements – A Management Guide (English)
- Frameworks for IT Management (English)

Pocket guides
- ISO/IEC 20000 – a pocket guide (English, German, Italian, Spanish, formerly BS 15000 – a pocket guide)
- IT Services Procurement based on ISPL – a pocket guide (English)
- IT Governance – a pocket guide based on COBIT (English, German)
- IT Service CMM – a pocket guide (English)
- IT Service Management – a summary based on ITIL® (Dutch)
- IT Service Management from hell! (English)

For any further enquiries about ITSM Library, please visit www.itsmfbooks.com, http://en.itsmportal.net/books.php?id=35 or www.vanharen.net.

Contents

Introduction

This book is founded on research conducted at Rhodes University into Service Management and Service Agreements. The initial prompting for this research came from one of the industry partners of the Distributed Multimedia Centre of Excellence. They expressed difficulty in the development and management of Service Level Agreements.

The initial explorations of the subject matter lead the researchers into a cauldron of misinformation, hype and vendor specific promotional literature. It was decided therefore to define the concepts, processes and terms involved in a Service Management (SM) initiative using as wide a range of sources as possible. The results of this are the working definitions that underpin this book.

It is important to realise that this is not an ITIL® book. The ITIL® framework is just one of many approaches that were used to develop the framework and model in this book that were then tested empirically in the research. Not every reader will be from an ITIL® background and although it is one of the better (and more comprehensive) frameworks at the moment, this book is designed specifically to be useful to all SM practitioners.

The authors encountered little consistency in the SM discipline as to the correct terminology and exactly what each term meant. The terms we use in the book, being Service Management (SM), Service Agreement (SA), Service Level Agreement (SLA) and Service Level Management (SLM) were chosen as they were the most common. Additionally, SM and SA were chosen above SLM and SLA as they downplay the importance of the "level" (the measure and hold accountable parts). While the authors recognise that "level" is important, but not nearly as important as the AGREEMENT part.

Service Management and Service Level Management are terms that are used interchangeably by practitioners. The same applies to Service Agreement and Service Level Agreement. For the purposes of this book, SM is seen to refer to a holistic strategy that covers all aspect of managing services. SLM therefore describes the management of a specific service to a specific level. The same distinction can be drawn between SA and SLA. An SA is seen as a single document that accommodates all that is relevant to an agreed business relationship. An SLA represents the documentation of that which is relevant to a level of service assigned to a particular business process or activity. An SA can therefore contain any number of individual SLAs.

An SA can be regarded as a Service Contract as it encapsulates all that which is relevant to the relationship between the service provider and the customer. For the sake of uniformity this book works from the view that there is a commercial business relationship between the service provider and the customer. Service Agreements can of course also be applied in non-commercial relationships. Internal service providers and their internal customers often prefer that. Whether such partners use formal or less formal agreements is depending upon the choice of the organisation. Whether the make-or-buy decision lead to formal outsourcing arrangements or not, in all cases the situation of a service provider, providing services to a customer, remains.

Any additional contracts that are negotiated between the service provider and the customer, with additional providers and/or vendors, are regarded as Underpinning Contracts (UCs). These UCs therefore bear reference on the relationship between the service provider and the customer.

Using this terminology this book lays out the fundamentals of an SM strategy. It describes in more detail, the contents of, and how to develop, the major parts of this strategy. Follow these guidelines and your SM initiative is far more likely to be successful.

CHAPTER 1

A Service Management Overview

The Information and Communication Technology (ICT) sector continues to experience evolutionary change, as it redefines itself after the well publicised stock market crash of the late 1990's. This crash occurred at a time when ICT initiatives were characterised by 'over-promise and under-deliver'. Many organisations lost a great deal of money, having invested heavily in ICT services that were unable to meet or satisfy their requirements. Consequently, organisations are now demanding improvements in the quality of the services delivered by ICT service providers, and decrease of cost. This demand for improvements in services applies to both outsourced and in-sourced (internal provided) ICT services.

In an attempt to improve service levels, service providers and customers are entering into Service Agreements (SAs). In some cases, organisations are drafting agreements with their own internal ICT departments. In other cases, organisations are outsourcing their ICT service provision to third parties. Either way, the management of service levels is of pivotal importance.

Unfortunately, many of these service provision initiatives either fail, or do not result in improvements in service levels. Service Management (SM) helps deliver improvements by providing an integrated approach to the management of ICT service requirements and levels.

1.1 Managing Service Levels

Business relationships involving the trading of services require mechanisms that manage the levels of service. While acceptable service levels promote further business interactions, poor service levels are likely to have a negative influence on the relationships between service provider and customer. This could result in the termination of the affected relationship. If the provided services do not meet the customer's expectations, further transactions between the two parties are unlikely to occur. Ensuring that services meet, and perhaps exceed, the customer's expectations, requires accurate and constant management. Further trading of services is negatively affected if the management of those service levels is deficient or absent. In today's ICT environments the offering of services with agreed service levels has become essential.

Before service levels can be managed, they have to be set. In order to establish service levels, the customer's expectations and the provider's capabilities need to be aligned. This process also requires the acknowledgement of the provider's capacity to provide services, the identification of the customer's requirements and then the marrying of these in an environment that promotes the development of a sustainable business relationship.

Additionally, in order to manage service levels, a mutual undertaking to develop the foundations of a partnership between service provider and customer, that meets the needs of both parties, is required. This undertaking serves to develop the foundations upon which an initial service provision can develop into a sustainable business relationship. The effective management of service levels is therefore of fundamental importance in any business relationship that is based on the sustained trading of services.

1.2   Definitions of Service Management

There are a number of definitions of SM. These many definitions show how broad the area of SM is. These definitions originate from a focus on the services, the customer or the provider.

With the focus on services, SM is seen as the process of negotiation, SA articulation and development, provision of checks and balances, and reviews between provider and customer regarding the services and service levels that support the customer's business process. In light of this, an SA is seen as a contract between a provider and a customer that documents the business processes as well as the supporting services, service parameters, acceptable / unacceptable service levels and liabilities on the part of the provider and the customer, and actions to be taken in specified circumstances. SM is therefore seen as the process of identifying, defining, negotiating, agreeing, implementing, monitoring, reporting and managing the levels of customer service, with the targets being documented in SAs.

With a customer focus, SM involves the definition of customer expectations, the satisfying of those expectations and the perpetual refining of the business agreement. SM is therefore seen as the process of setting, measuring and ensuring the maintenance of service goals. SM helps organisations make sure that their key targets for service success are being met. SM is a process for delivering services that constantly meet the customer's requirements. Performance management is a key function of SM and this includes the definition, measurement and assessment of services, as well as the setting and monitoring of service objectives and service levels. Allied to these function are the associated activities of reporting, customer interaction, Customer Relationship Management (CRM) and negotiating SAs. Good SM leads to the refinement and improvement of services. A further benefit of managing service levels involves gaining customer loyalty and trust. In order to do so, the managing of relationships with customers is an integral part of SM.

From a service provider's perspective, SM can be seen as a set of people and systems that allow the organisation to ensure that agreed service levels are being met and that the necessary resources are being provided efficiently. This relationship exists between people and systems, but systems further separates into technology or tools and processes.

SM is therefore seen by the provider as a disciplined, proactive methodology used to ensure that required levels of service are delivered to customers in accordance with business priorities and at acceptable cost.

In practice the focus on services, customer or provider, depends on the actual business strategy. For instance, a corporate focus on maximum customer satisfaction may result in a service management focus on the customer, whereas a corporate focus on cost saving may result in a service management focus on measurable and matching services.

For the purposes of this book, SM is defined as follows:

> SM is a cyclical and collaborative process. It is initiated by the verification of the service provider's capacity to deliver and manage services according to identified service levels. This is followed by a process of the understanding and defining a customer's requirements, the negotiating, creating, deploying and refining SAs and the real-time monitoring and reporting of service levels. This is done within a framework of accountable costs, continual service level improvements and perpetual development of the business relationship.

1.3 Elements of Service Management

The primary goal of every ICT service provider should be to provide services that are aligned with and support an organisation's business strategy and objectives. Since many of today's businesses operate in a dynamic environment, this goal has become increasingly elusive. The only way ICT service providers can continue to hit the moving target of supporting business needs is by having an SM strategy in place.

While SM is an overriding process, it has six key elements:
- Service Agreements (SAs)
- Operational Level Agreements (OLAs)
- Underpinning Contracts (UCs)
- Reporting
- Service Catalogue
- Technology and toolsets.

1.3.1 Service Agreements

An SA is a legally binding document between the service provider and the customer that specifies the expectations and obligations that exist in a business relationship between them. SAs are therefore contracts between service providers and customers that define:
- The services to be provided
- The metrics associated with these services
- The acceptable and unacceptable service levels
- The liabilities and obligations on the part of the service provider and customer
- The actions to be taken in specific circumstances.

The term 'Service Level Agreement' is used variably, including referring to the whole SA. This could be somewhat confusing and misleading. The expression 'Service Level Agreement' places the emphasis on the level at which the services are to be provided. It often happens that other important contractual and commercial/business issues (and their legal ramifications) are overlooked.

Roles of a Service Agreement

Although an SA is an excellent expectations-management mechanism, it is important to manage the expectations of what the SA can realistically accomplish. An SA is frequently incorrectly viewed as a complaint-stifling mechanism or a quick fix to a troubled relationship; however, using it for such purpose creates more problems than it solves. Instead, an SA should be viewed as:
- *A communications tool* - The value of an agreement is not just in the final product; the very process of establishing an SA helps to open up communications.
- *A conflict-prevention tool* - An agreement helps to avoid or alleviate disputes by providing a shared understanding of needs and priorities. If conflicts do occur, they tend to be resolved more readily and with less damage to the relationship.
- *A living document* - An SA is not a dead-end document meant to be filed and forgotten. At a pre-determined frequency, the parties to the SA review the agreement to assess service adequacy and negotiate adjustments. This is one of its most important benefits.

- *An objective basis for gauging service effectiveness* - An SA ensures that both parties use the same criteria to evaluate service quality.

An SA is an agreement between the customer and the service provider that quantifies the minimum acceptable levels of services required by the customer. An SA is probably the most important document in a service provider/customer relationship. An SA, when properly written, is distinguished by clear, simple language and focuses on the needs of the customer's organisation. Creating a sound, mutually agreeable SA is a matter of appropriate diligence by both parties.

Content of a Service Agreement
SAs include the following:
- A description of the services that shall to be provided
- The expected performance from those services
- A detailed procedure for handling service degradations
- A procedure for monitoring and reporting the service levels to the customer
- The pricing of the services
- The consequences of the service provider not meeting the agreed service levels and of the customer not fulfilling their obligations
- A description of under which circumstances the SA does not apply.

The parties involved in the development of an SA should be concerned with at least the following points:
- A description of the services that are to be provided
  - What is included and what is excluded
  - When the SA comes into effect
  - The validity period of the SA.
  - Frequency of review/amendments
  - Scheduled (operational, tactical and strategic) meetings between service provider and customer
  - Is there need for an installation timetable
- The expected performance of the services
  - Does this include routine maintenance and customer induced outages
  - Network-based availability or site-based availability
  - How is performance measured (throughput, loss, downtime, etc)
  - Who monitors the hardware (customer or service provider)
  - When does a service degradation start counting? When it is reported, confirmed, or detected
  - Confidentiality clauses

- A detailed procedure for handling services degradations
  - Feedback
  - Contact people - who to call about what
  - Mean time to respond
  - Mean time to repair
  - Remember - compensation is not the reason for service agreements
- A procedure for monitoring and reporting the service levels to the customer
  - How will the services be monitored
  - How useful is the reporting
    - Interpretation of the reports and statistics
    - Detail the process for the gathering of data as well as any gaps in the data
    - Suggestions for optimisation (capital investment, bandwidth, heavy users or applications)
    - Warning indication of degradation before it becomes a service degradation
- The consequences of the service provider diverging from the agreed service levels
  - Rewards and/or penalties
  - Can a financial penalty compensate for lost customers
  - Termination conditions
  - Repeated breaches of target service levels - implement a chronic service failure termination right
- A description of under which circumstances the SLAs in an SA do not apply
  - Earthquakes, floods or terrorism for example.

Structure of a Service Agreement

To be effective, an SA must incorporate two sets of elements, namely, management elements and service elements. Management elements are issues such as reporting, regular meetings, conflict alleviation and delivery monitoring. Service elements include items such as precise Service Level Agreements (SLAs) about specific services. These two elements can be included in two ways:

1. The management elements for the relevant services are contained in the Master Services Agreement and the quantification of the service is contained in an Operational SA or
2. Both are contained in a single SA.

The management and service elements are sometimes classified as Agreement clauses and Schedules respectively. This classification is very similar, as described below.

Ideally, the Agreement clauses serve a number of very useful functions:

- They set out the framework or structure of the Agreement, and the core issues, in a comprehensive, logical and easily understandable manner.
- They set out the management structures and arrangements that are put in place by the parties to oversee the service provision activities and which provide a focal point for issues such as change control and dispute resolution.
- They contain the interpretation provision which collects all the defined terms that are used throughout the SA.
- They contain a summary of the major obligations of both parties.
- They describe the financial arrangements that are to apply for the duration of the contract.
- They set out the warranties that will be applicable.
- They deal with the liability regime that is to apply across the entire SA.
- They set out the dispute resolution process or procedures that are to apply.
- They address in detail the intellectual property issues that are relevant to the transaction.
- They describe the termination and disengagement arrangements that are such an important feature of outsourcing arrangements.

The Schedules are traditionally used to include high level detail about particular aspects of, or arrangements under, the SA. Schedules therefore usually contain:

- Details of the services to be provided
- Details of the levels at which the services are to be provided
- Lists of equipment that exists, that which is to be sold, that which is to be leased and that which is to be provided to the service provider
- Lists of the software owned by the customer and owned by third parties that is to be used in the provision of the services
- List of rates that will be applicable to the provision of specified services (usually by reference to a particular classification of employee of the service provider)
- Details of the service fees to be paid, the dates on which these are to be paid and other details associated with the price and payment arrangements
- Relevant plans (for example, plans for transition, quality, management and disaster recovery)
- Deed of guarantee
- And many others - depending on the nature and size of the transaction.

The SLA is that part of the SA that defines the services to be provided and the levels at which the services are to be provided. Not only are there different models for SAs, there are also different models used for constructing an SLA. An SLA comprises the following components:

- **Statement of work** - This part of the SA defines the types of services that are to be performed by the service provider.
- **Service level details** - This part of the SA quantifies the services that are to be provided (service levels) and the measures used to assess how the services are being provided.
- **Description of roles and responsibilities** - This part of the SA sets out the roles and the responsibilities of the customer and the service provider and makes it clear who is accountable for ensuring that the statement of work and the service levels are maintained.
- **Reporting procedures** - This part of the SA defines the reporting arrangements and reporting deliverables that are required from the service provider.

SLAs are one of the most important aspects of an SA. SLAs define the level of service that is to be provided, as agreed to by the parties involved. These are explained in the context of business goals and contain one or more service level indicators (Slips).

If an SA is going to be valuable, it must contain SLAs, which should:
- Identify what aspects of service are covered by the agreement
- Define the target level for each aspect of service
- Identify Slips for each aspect of service
- Relate to specific business objectives.

Each aspect of an SLA, such as service availability, must have a target level of achievement. However the agreement might include two measures for each aspect: a minimum acceptable level of service to achieve, and a desired level of service that the service provider should aim to achieve and for which a reward can be given. Planners should aim for between 5 and 10 SLAs per SA, with the goal of keeping it simple.

Slips are at the heart of an SA. They allow the service provision to be measured and quantified. Typical metrics are a percentage of time available, or level of performance for a single aspect of a single type of technology also soft aspects as customer satisfaction might be measured' in between the words. Ideally, Slips should:
- Allow quality to be quantified
- Reflect users' pain points/priorities
- Include availability, performance, and accuracy metrics

- Take into account security features and systems
- Be affordable.

The best way to measure service levels is from the customer's perspective. Aspects to measure include how available and how responsive the services were. Whichever way this is measured, the SA needs to document each SLI used to measure the objectives, and to specify the data source for each. Customers need to determine the most critical aspects of a service and then to ensure that SLAs are defined and negotiated to address them. Critical aspects include service security, service levels, service response times, infrastructure uptime/downtime, network performance, backup and disaster recovery, scalability, reporting, customer and customer satisfaction, overall end-to-end performance of service features, and escalation processes.

Service Agreement Life Cycle

The life cycle of an SA is delineated into the following stages:

- Creation Phase
- Operation Phase
- Removal Phase

Depending on the business scenario, each phase may consist of many sub phases. Additionally, some provisioning activity (putting processes and assets in place to offer the service) may take place prior to creation of an SA, and/or deferred until runtime invocation of a service.

Creation Phase

An SA is first created when a customer subscribes to, or seeks to purchase, a service that is offered by a service provider. A (possibly complex) chain of events leads to the point where the customer wants to subscribe to the service. The customer would first have found out about the existence of the service offering, and gathered enough detailed information about this offering to judge if it is a service that the customer wants. The customer might have been actively searching for a service offering to support an already identified business need.

SA creation involves two activities:

- **Development of the SA** - This reflects that the customer has actually subscribed to the service and is aware of the detailed legally binding extent of what is comprised in the service delivery. The customer has copies of all relevant information about the service. In this step the customer signs a service delivery contract.

- **Preparing the service provision** - All required service subsystems need to be configured to accommodate this new service subscription. This includes access authorisation systems for the service, entries into billing systems, entries into the service logic of the service, reservations of required and per-customer service resources, for example.

The SA creation phase is usually also an input into longer term resource planning activities for the service provider.

Operational Phase

During the provision of a service, a service provider monitors the service level as per the associated SA with the customer and actively manages resources to avoid any violation of identified, defined and agreed levels of service. This includes prioritisation of requests, based on service level assessment, and/or dynamic allocation of resources by assigning a thread priority. The service provider also controls customer access to a service so that it does not exceed the guaranteed throughput level.

A customer may also monitor the levels of received services to avoid any blind trust on a service provider. In some scenarios, the two parties may agree to use an independent third-party for monitoring service levels. Obviously, this is possible if the third-party can independently measure the service levels either via special probe transactions, or by receiving raw performance data from multiple sources (customer and service provider for example).

Any violation of guarantees are noted for future penalty assessment and/or dynamically notified to the parties to the agreement. Upon identifying a violation, the customer may choose to terminate its SA with the service provider. The service provider may use this violation (as well as alerts on potential future violations) to dynamically provide new resources. When a service provider is not able to meet all its commitments, it may prioritise its business commitments using various business objectives (for example, profit maximisation, preferential treatment of loyal customers) and in the worst scenarios terminate certain SAs.

Removal Phase

An SA specifies a validity period, after which the service provision detailed in the SA is terminated. The SA may also be terminated explicitly either by the customer or the service provider (due to the change in requirements of a customer and/or capability of the service provider). The business and legal implications of such a termination is outside the scope of this book. The termination may also be initiated as a result of multiple/excessive violations of guaranteed service levels specified in the SA. Finally, an SA may be renegotiated to extend the validity period, and/or agree on a new service levels and price.

1.3.2 Operational Level Agreements

SAs are not enough to ensure the timely delivery of service as needed by the business. Operational Level Agreements (OLAs) need to be put in place between related ICT departments in order to unify ICT service delivery throughout an organisation prior to executing customer SAs.

OLAs establish specific technical, informational, and timeframe requirements needed for each ICT department to provide the services that will be delivered to the customer. For example, the email administrator might require specific information, as well as a 48-hour span of time to create an email box for a new employee. This needs to be documented and approved by all impacted ICT departments before the Service Desk establishes an email provisioning SA with the customer.

Without OLAs in place, SAs will frequently promise services that are impractical at best or impossible at worst. Clearly defined OLAs prevent un-kept promises to customers. Additionally, OLAs present a more united ICT service provider to the customer. On many occasions, the exercise of building thorough OLAs can iron out long-standing feuds that have been based on misunderstandings. Ultimately, OLAs hold each group accountable for their service, and also build understanding of each group's contribution to the overall delivery of service.

Key performance objectives and internal incentives need to directly relate to OLA compliance. Since the entire goal of an ICT service provider is to service the customer, well-defined OLAs should provide a template of objectives that show managers those activities that are most appropriate to monitor, report, and reward.

Lastly, OLAs need to serve as a benchmark any time SAs need to flex to meet business requirements. If a specific service is required faster or differently by a business unit, the OLAs show exactly which groups need to be consulted, and which services provided by those groups ultimately affect the delivery of the desired service. If the providing group can agree to change how their service is delivered, then the SA can be changed, and the OLA can be altered accordingly.

1.3.3   Underpinning Contracts

For any services provided by third-party vendors or service providers, Underpinning Contracts (UCs) need to be put in place. UCs are similar to OLAs in that they complete the chain of accountability and control for seamless service delivery. ICT service organisations may put contractual agreements in place with their third-party vendors, and convert the pertinent data into a UC that complements their entire SM process. As service needs change with the business units, ICT Service providers negotiate any changes with third-party vendors as needed, and modify the UC accordingly.

1.3.4   Reporting

Reporting efforts need to complement the key measurements in SAs, OLAs, and UCs. Reports that show the overall SM performance must be communicated upward to ICT management, as well as to the customer's management. Effective SM reporting demonstrates the value of ICT and business alignment. A thorough understanding of ICT service capabilities can help guide business planning. Conversely, ICT can scale back or enhance services to meet business needs in future. Additionally, effective performance reporting is an excellent management tool, as well as providing performance incentives to staff. When you are measuring and reporting the right things, performance reporting can efficiently modify service behaviour, provide incentive, and reward the achievers in a consistent fashion throughout ICT. The net result is a more satisfied and effective workforce.

1.3.5   Service Catalogue

In the same way a restaurant menu sets initial expectations for a customer and provides the basis for personalised service, the Service Catalogue enables ICT organisations to market and commit to achievable levels of service at a predictable cost or planned price. A Service Catalogue clearly defines what services are available from the ICT service provider and aligns those services with business goals and needs. The Service Catalogue focuses specifically on documenting and articulating all the ICT services provided by the organisation. This includes the necessary service requirements that are usually detailed in an SA. However, at its simplest level, a Service Catalogue is a record of all the services offered within the organisation that will contribute to the success of SM. With this focus in mind, a Service Catalogue is developed in order to do or support the following:

- Define and publish all available ICT services and SAs provided by the service provider that align with business needs
- Standardise service fulfilment processes
- Establish achievable service levels
- Determine the associated costs
- Manage performance.

From a high level perspective, the objective of SM is to lead ICT service providers through the design of a Service Catalogue, the development of detailed service descriptions for their services, and the development of an SA for their major, mission-critical services that are well-defined, measurable, and in a negotiable state. These services are then documented in a Service Catalogue.

From an ICTSM maturity perspective, the goals of an organization using a Service Catalogue are to:
- Detail an inventory of all ICT services that are provided by the service provider
- Enable an optimised, service focused organisation
- Describe and document a well-defined and effective set of tailored processes and methods that are supported organisation-wide and are continuously improved
- Provide an integrated set of people, process, and technology that is well-established, can be integrated into the organisation, organisation-wide, and continuously improved as needed.

Specifically, one area that denotes SM maturity within ICTSM is the development and maintenance of a Service Catalogue that includes identifying and qualifying the types of services being provided and integrating Service Level Objectives (SLOs) and agreements information that employs a business and customer service focus.

1.3.6 Technology and Toolsets

Since SM is almost entirely based upon processes, many ICT service managers make the mistake of assuming that SM can be done manually and through effective communications alone. This is a mistake and a common reason why SM initiatives fail. SM is an ICT organisation-wide initiative that is much too complex to monitor and maintain manually. The flow of data alone is much more than can be handled manually. Appropriate SM creates a stream of data that shows the flow of every service transaction through the SM process. The levels of service are then compared with the SA, OLA, and UC, where appropriate, and the pertinent data of the event is logged for reporting.

An SM tool provides analytical data to analyze the environment on a real-time basis and raise alerts when service levels are in danger of slipping lower than the agreed-upon levels both for incidents measured individually and multiple incidents measured cumulatively over time. The benefits of SM are virtually amputated if it is implemented manually. Inferior enabling technology is a key delaying point for a successful implementation of SM. A robust toolset (including those for reporting), however, paves the way for the provider organisation to manage services.

1.4 The Importance of Service Management

For the improvement of ICT services, effective SM is a matter of survival. SM benefits the customer, the ICT service provider and the corporations in which they each work. SM can temper the customer's demands for a higher level of service, as well as hold ICT service providers accountable for delivering agreed levels of service. Recognising that outsourcing continues to be popular, SM can be a defensive strategy, against which, the customer dissatisfaction that leads to outsourcing, can be negated. The following are six reasons why SM is important:

1.4.1 Customer Satisfaction
Customer satisfaction is the foremost reason for implementing SM as it:
- Necessitates dialogue between ICT managers and their customers
- Forces customers to state clearly their requirements and expectations
- Sets benchmarks when customer and provider agree on acceptable service levels
- Establishes dialogue channels which lead to improved reporting.

SM cannot produce happy customers when service level commitments are not met. However SM does significantly raise the overall levels of customer satisfaction when commitments are met, and helps to improve the situation when targets are missed.

1.4.2 Managing Expectations
The use of best practice SM can reduce or avoid mismatched expectations and scope creep. Effective documentation of customer requirements in the SA helps to manage customer expectations, and provides clear statements of situations when the SA would require re-negotiation.

1.4.3 Resource Regulation
SM provides a form of governance over ICT resources, recognising that monitoring of services, by both customer and service provider, to maintain the SAs, ensures early warning for any change in capacity that might be required.

1.4.4 Internal Marketing of ICT Services
When used correctly, SM not only helps ICT departments to deploy resources fairly, but can also be a great marketing tool. By ensuring ongoing, consistent levels of response time and availability, SAs provide a powerful way for ICT service providers to inform customers of their good service levels. In doing so, they suggest that SM takes ICT out of the category of liability and puts it amongst the company's assets.

1.4.5 Cost Control

In terms of cost control, SM can be a double-edged sword. SM can help service providers more accurately determine the true costs of service provision, removing the guesswork which often leads to excess and unjustified costs. It can also help the customer and service provider to understand the true cost of the required service levels, and facilitates informed business decision making to allow the appropriate balance of cost and quality.

1.4.6 Defensive Strategy

ICT managers, like everyone, are motivated by self-interest, suggesting that it is clearly in the interests of ICT managers to implement an SM process. With SM in place, ICT service providers have a tool to use in defending themselves from customer attacks. Clear documentation, well written SAs and metrics for measuring service levels remove any doubt as to whether or not objectives have been met.

SM is the continuous process of measuring, reporting, and improving the quality of service provided by ICT to the business. In order to do this, the ICT service provider is required to understand each service it provides, including relative priorities, business importance, and which lines of business and individual users consume which service. The primary consideration is to ensure that the service levels to be managed are measured and evaluated from a perspective that matches the business goals of the organisation.

1.5 The Benefits of Service Management

Improvements in service quality and reductions in service degradations as a result of effective SM can ultimately lead to significant financial savings. Less time and effort is spent by ICT staff in resolving fewer failures and ICT customers are able to perform their business functions without adverse impact. The following are key benefits of SM:

- ICT services are designed to meet service level requirements.
- Improved relationships are fostered with satisfied customers.
- Both parties to the agreement have a clearer view of roles and responsibilities, avoiding potential misunderstandings or omissions.
- Specific targets are noted, against which service quality can be measured, monitored and reported.
- ICT effort is focused on business priorities.
- ICT and customers have a clear and consistent expectation of the level of service required.
- Service monitoring allows weak areas to be identified, so that remedial action can be taken, thus improving future service quality.

- Service monitoring also shows where customer actions are causing the fault and so identify where working efficiency and/or training can be improved.
- SM underpins provider management.
- In some cases where services are outsourced, the SAs are a key part of managing the relationship with the third-party. In other cases, service monitoring allows the performance of providers to be evaluated and managed.
- An SA is used as a basis for charging and helps demonstrate what value customers are receiving for their money.

The cumulative effect of the benefits listed above leads to a gradual improvement in service quality and an overall reduction in the cost of service provision. In addition, SM establishes, and keeps open, regular lines of communication between service providers and customers. The beneficial impact of this should not be underestimated.

There are five groups of SM benefits; business, financial, employee, innovation and internal.

1.5.1   Business Benefits
The business benefits centre on the improvements in the quality, reliability and predictability of business operations. This leads to better working relationships and satisfaction between customer and provider.

1.5.2   Financial Benefits
Long term financial benefits are associated with a cost-justified ICT infrastructure. These include improved reaction time, preventative measures and service continuity expenditure.

1.5.3   Employee Benefits
Employees have clearer role definitions. They experience increased motivation, job satisfaction and increased productivity. The ICT provider's reputation can also improve.

1.5.4   Innovation Benefits
The clearer understanding of ICT requirements and service levels provides for greater flexibility and adaptability within services. Improvements are noticeable in the ability to recognise changing trends and to adapt quickly to new requirements and market developments.

1.5.5 Internal Benefits

Associated with the improved metrics and management reporting are the improvements in information and its communication to decision makers. Clearer role definition and view of current ICT capabilities lead to process maturity, providing repeatable, consistent and self-improving benefits.

1.5.6 Quantifying the Benefits of Service Management

In quantifying the effects when ICT resources fail or are inaccessible, a corresponding loss of business revenue usually occurs. The associated lost opportunity costs are also accompanied by other losses due to regulatory penalties and market share loss to competitors. It is also important to consider that the cost of downtime varies significantly by industry, acknowledging that financial services companies have extremely high costs associated with even the smallest disruption in service.

In quantifying the impact on business revenue, an understanding of the critical business systems and the associated revenue gained by those systems on an annual basis is required. This information can then be extrapolated to an hourly rate, and by assessing the increased service availability due to proactive SM, a corresponding benefit can be calculated.

SM benefits can also be demonstrated by showing the direct impact of outages and service degradations on end users, demonstrations of which also include the additional time that users are productive based on the increased availability. These improved productivity calculations and forecasts can further strengthen the case for proactive SM.

Potential SM implementers can also use their newly acquired data on future business applications, workloads and service levels to forecast the necessary ICT architecture and assets needed to deliver on those requirements. This guarantees that adequate capacity will be available and also supports a policy of just-in-time upgrades. This approach helps deliver better return on capital employed, recognising that the net present value of deferring hardware purchases can be calculated along with any associated costs for maintenance charges for upgrading software licenses.

Proactive SM also leads to higher utilisation levels of ICT components because of more accurate service quality measurement and the ability to balance workloads more efficiently across available resources. These improved levels of utilisation permit ICT service providers to defer the need for upgrading hardware and software. Being proactive can also encompass monitoring the service to anticipate and prevent service degradations.

True SM means going beyond the historical and reactive aspects of the process, suggesting that it requires becoming proactive and focusing on continuous service improvements. Being proactive means that an ICT service provider:

- Has developed a thorough, tested, comprehensive program for backup and recovery, including complete and tested disaster recovery
- Monitors the service to anticipate and prevent service degradations
- Thoroughly controls the flow of demands for the service.

The benefits of a successfully implemented SM strategy are clearly evident for both the customer and the provider. These benefits relate to the improvements in communication between customers and providers, increased levels of service and the refining of business practices. Employees of both the provider and customer organisations experience increased productivity and motivation. These benefits of SM can be grouped into two broad categories:

- **Improved Customer Relationship Management** - SM leads to improvements in managing and satisfaction of the customer's expectations. An effective SM strategy includes the relevant planning, procedures and practices that focus on the customer and the satisfaction of their expectations.
- **Improved Business Practices** - SM provides a framework for improving service quality and reducing costs. The process also empowers ICT staff, as the focus on SM improves the marketing of the ICT services. It further facilitates an organisation's ability to respond resourcefully to the dynamic ICT environment.

It is clear that the reasons to implement an SM framework are substantial. The case for SM is convincing for both the provider and the customer. The benefits of a successful SM program will ultimately impact on the bottom lines of the companies who implement it successfully. The improvements in customer relationships, the reduced costs and the improved business practices have significant financial benefits.

1.6 Return on Investments in Service Management Solutions

ICT service providers face multiple challenges in ensuring the delivery of services across the networked infrastructure. In order to recognise the return on an investment in managing service levels, consider the following key issues:

- Customer satisfaction and loyalty
- Productivity
- Proactive planning
- Costs associated with Service Management implementation.

1.6.1　Customer Satisfaction and Loyalty

Given the increased levels of competition facilitated by the internet, the focus within ICT has shifted from improving the effectiveness within the corporation to improving the efficiencies as they apply to the corporation's supply chain. Customer satisfaction and loyalty are areas that are increasingly more important for many organisations and service providers. Many providers are attempting to build relationships with their key customers that are more than just a provider and customer relationship.

It is recognised that these newly found partnerships bring new challenges. A shift has occurred from improving the effectiveness within the corporation to improving efficiencies and effectiveness of a corporation's supply chain, sale channels and marketing efforts. This shift provides the service provider with the daunting task of ensuring that their solutions deliver against the requirements of all the businesses involved, as opposed to an application, server or group with the organisation.

1.6.2　Productivity

Service degradation or outage influences the amount of time end users can work as well as their ability of a user to perform their tasks efficiently and productively. Work outages are both costly and time consuming. It takes an average of 20 minutes for an end user to get to where they were before the application failed. Such degradations in service, commonly referred to as brownouts, occur more frequently than total service outages, and range from slowdowns to unacceptable response times. Quantifying the impact of brownouts drives home the importance of properly implemented service management. This results in significant savings being realised if degradations and outages are minimised or eliminated all together.

1.6.3　Proactive Planning

Planning is needed, in terms of capacity and future business applications, to ensure that the demands of the customer community are met.

Many providers in the marketplace tout their proactive approach towards service management, which involves bringing visibility to the future needs or future problems of an organisation. Future needs can be identified and defined by understanding prospective business applications and workloads, as well as the services required to deliver these to the end user. The result of this proactive approach enables end users to ensure that adequate capacity is available when the need arises. Service providers are also aware that being proactive in understanding when services will breach thresholds, allows end users to correct issues before they impact productivity and ultimately revenue. In doing so, this approach will allow for a more efficient use of capital and resources and can result in a planned approach to investing in ICT.

A proactive SM strategy offers a number of benefits to consider when calculating the return on investment and investment versus benefits. With SM, organisations will better understand the quality of the service it provides to end users and to the various lines of business. In addition, SM can help ICT service providers to optimise the service it provides to customers by automating and centralising the control of business-critical applications and the underlying components, such as databases, server operating systems, middleware, networks and server hardware.

SM enables ICT service providers to show increased business revenue, as a function of reducing outages and improving ICT service providers performance that directly affect business operations. Recognising that SM methods require ICT service providers to collect user and departmental requirements with appropriate diligence, SM assists ICT service providers forecasting and planning. This in order to meet future workload volumes and required service levels for seasonal, geographic or application-related variations in overall traffic loads. These same measured loads can also be better balanced and distributed amongst existing resources, getting the maximum use of existing components while still meeting service level requirements.

For carriers and service providers, SM can reduce or eliminate the penalties associated with broken contractual commitments, achieving and sustaining better availability and performance. SM leads to increases in shareholder value, and helps eliminate headline grabbing outages that erode investor confidence. Recognising that improved reliability can also translate into a competitive advantage, service providers should approach SM with rigor.

With SM, organisations can reduce the incidence of lost revenue, either because internal transactions could not be completed, or because external customers could not access electronic catalogues or shopping carts. SM ensures that business units or departments with more time-intensive ICT requirements pay accordingly, without relegating more strategic areas or functions to second-class status or endangering a smooth flow of business operation.

1.6.4   The Costs Associated with Service Management Implementation

There are four main areas where costs are incurred in implementing Service Management. These relate to ICT Personnel, Software, Hardware and Management.

ICT Personnel

The costs of ICT personnel to plan, implement, monitor and report against agreed SAs.

Software Costs

The software costs incurred by developing the necessary tools to monitor, diagnose, manage, and report service quality, including the notification of service issues.

Additional Hardware

The costs related to any additional hardware, whether for more servers, workstations and/or specialised equipment for supporting SM.

ICT Management Overhead

The costs incurred by ICT management in justifying SM to executive management, the procurement of software and hardware, recruiting and training ICT personnel and overseeing the SM function.

1.7   Current Service Management Problems

Unfortunately, many SM initiatives fail. Failure can be attributed to a number of factors, most prominent of which is the lack of knowledge and understanding that plagues SM. A number of problem areas impact negatively on SM, mostly concentrated around the confusion surrounding the use and value of SM, the inappropriate application of SM, the manner in which services are measured and managed and the lack of skilled practitioners in the field.

1.7.1   Misinformation and Misunderstanding

While the benefits of integrated management of service levels are significant, the foundations on which they are built are increasingly fractured and lacking in standards support. While SM, including Quality of Service (QoS), SAs and service assurance, are currently topical in ICT circles, a great deal of misinformation surrounds the topic. The cause of this misinformation and misunderstanding stem from five SM myths:

Myth 1: SA equals SM
Managers often mistakenly assume that SM is the same as SA. SM can be successful without SAs, yet, on the other hand, SAs in the absence of SM are meaningless.

Myth 2: SAs will make users happy
SAs are not a magic potion, an SA is a way to set expectations and communicate about the services that are being delivered.

Myth 3: SAs will result in higher service levels
By itself, an SA can not directly produce any changes in the levels of service delivery. However, improvements in service levels sometimes coincide with the establishment of SAs. This is due to the paying of closer attention to services and the improvements in customer/service provider communication during the negotiation phase. An SM program is the reason for any resulting increases in levels of service.

Myth 4: Penalty clauses in an SA will guarantee service levels
Penalty clauses act as incentives to service providers as well as define appropriate compensation when service levels are not met. However, it is very difficult to negotiate penalty clauses that meet these two objectives. Difficulty exists in extracting these penalties without the assistance of costly legal action.

Myth 5: SAs are not necessary when outsourcing ICT functions
Many companies do not have SAs with their outsourcing partners. This level of trust is both naïve and could be considered as negligence on the part of the managers.

1.7.2   Developing Service Agreements
Developing SAs is a most difficult problem and must be addressed. SAs must be consistently and accurately defined, documented and monitored, with regular reviews. If not, then potential service improvements are not realised and SAs may fall into disuse. It is more difficult to resurrect them or to re-launch SM. Consequently, it is far better to recognise the potential difficulties in advance by putting correct development procedures in place.

SAs establish a negotiated and agreed upon two-way accountability for service. They build credibility for the service organisation by indicating how serious they are about providing support. Yet while many organisations understand the vital role played by SAs, many are unaware or unwilling to dedicate the amount of resources required to maintain them.

1.7.3 Reporting

Reporting efforts need to complement the important measurements in SAs. Reports that show the overall SM performance must be communicated to ICT management and ICT middle management, as well as to the customer's management structures. Effective SM reporting is the medium of communication that demonstrates the value of ICT and business alignment, serving as a management tool.

Reporting to customers about performance is a key monitoring aspect of SM. Unfortunately, much of today's ICT reporting is of limited worth as the associated reports are usually filled with technical data that has little, or no, value to the customer. Reporting can be done periodically or in real-time, the latter enjoying first priority. A critical aspect of SM failures is a lack of attention given to the development of reporting structures.

1.7.4 Semantic Disparity Problem

There are methods and challenges regarding SM, however, the crux of SM involves two competing strains, referred to as the semantic disparity problem:

- Parameters that are easy to measure for ICT specialists do not translate well into parameters that are readily understood by customers.
- Parameters that are easily understood by customers are not easy to measure for ICT specialists.

There is little new in this distinction, as Albert Einstein's originally observed that 'not everything that can be counted counts and not everything that counts can be counted'.

1.7.5 People Issues

People issues are a big challenge to implementing and improving SM. People issues include training, workflow and role definition, and management of change.

1.7.6 Fluid Business / Static Service

The business processes that are supported by services are in a state of constant flux. Yet the provider continues to offer the same services in the same way. The services offered previously may have become ill adjusted to the business needs, and/or have not kept pace with the change. The business, on the other hand, may have embarked on changes to stay competitive. The result has been a widening gap between the services offered and their usefulness to the business units.

1.7.7   Inefficient or Non-Existent Change Management

Change requests that come to ICT from the business units should be managed through a formal, customer-facing change management process. Often, however, internal ICT groups circumvented this formal process.

1.7.8   Disunity

A problem with change management is that it is often a symptom of a deeper cultural problem. Because there is no unified vision for ICT service and support, each group forms its own vision and ends up stepping on the vision and goals of the other groups. The result is that, over time, political barriers form that can lead to cumbersome procedures that are often burdened with a protective hidden agenda. As ICT groups hoard their knowledge, support often takes longer, and as a result, the true, united capabilities and service value of ICT are unknown to ICT or its customers.

1.7.9   The Deception of Customer Satisfaction

It is important to measure customer satisfaction at the service transaction level. This does not necessarily measure how well ICT services are aligned with business needs. Many ICT support managers have been deluded by good customer satisfaction scores that dismiss them from the hard work of forming true business alignment by engaging in continuous dialogue with their customers.

1.7.10   The Legacy of Failure

Many organisations can attest to failed ICT Service Agreements. In these organisations, SAs often took months to create. The customers are most cooperative in telling ICT service providers what they need, and the service provider creates the SAs. The results are documents that are somewhat complex, requiring work to monitor and maintain. Additionally, these agreements called for a system of measurements that are meaningful for the business units, but require data from the ICT service provider that is time consuming to assemble. Eventually these SAs are tossed in a drawer and became dead documents. They are not monitored, and no continuous feedback process, to stakeholders, is in place. The result is a lack of accountability between all those involved. ICT service providers must establish a link between service performance and business performance.

1.8   Successful Service Management

Where SM is defined as the process of managing customer expectations, no indication is given of how successful SM is identified. Unhappy customers, service failures, poor business relationships and poorly developed SAs would appear to be indicators of unsuccessful SM.

Successful SM involves the definition of customer expectations, the satisfying of those expectations and the perpetual refining of this business agreement. While this approach is pragmatic and simple, it does not provide sufficient insight into what a successful service management strategy is. There is credence to this pragmatic approach however, as it identifies services with respect to a customer and a provider. This approach additionally recommends the longevity of the association between customer and provider by recognising the need to perpetually refine the business agreement. Where this approach is lacking is in the articulation of what each of these entail.

The key indicators of successful SM are the continuous successful mapping of services to the ever changing customer requirements, the sustained provision of services, and a mutually beneficial customer/provider relationship under the umbrella of a shared strategy.

1.8.1   Successful Mapping of Services to Customer Requirements

A key ingredient of successfully providing services is recognising those services that can be provided and then mapping them to the customer's requirements. Successful service management ensures that ICT services are aligned to the business needs. This introspection is a fundamental building block of successful SM. A service provider who has not clearly identified and documented their service capabilities before attempting to map them to the customer's requirements is least likely to successfully manage those services.

1.8.2   Sustained Provision of Services

In order for provided services to be successful, they need to constantly satisfy the customer's requirements. If the requirements are not satisfied, then the provision of services is likely to be terminated. There is therefore a relationship between the successful service provision and the duration of the customer / provider relationship. That is to say, as long as customers are being provided with services that meet their requirements, they will remain satisfied. Conversely, if the provision of services is not sustained, then this could be representative of unsuccessful service management.

1.8.3   Mutually Beneficial Customer / Provider Relationship

The essence of the success of SM pivots around the nature of the relationship between customer and provider. Successful SM will be possible where this relationship has mutual benefit. Where benefit is mutual, the motivation to sustain the relationship is also mutual. This provides the foundation for a successful partnership built on a managed services environment.

1.8.4   Shared Strategy

An additional foundation stone of a successful SM environment is the presence of a shared strategy. Partnerships are built on a shared vision or strategy that unites the two parties. If the service provider and the customer share a common business strategy, the success of the managed services is likely to be more attainable.

1.9   A Framework for Service Management

Many organisations have been restructuring and reorganising in recent years in an effort to address the ICT resource and productivity issues they face. These issues are linked to the cost of ICT and the continual need to upgrade their systems, as well as systems uptime and reliability. Organisational effort is also being expended in order to absorb the new technologies required to run the services being developed. These activities will continue to increase in the future as a result of the e-services industry. None of these efforts produce the required infrastructure stability and performance needed to compete in the emerging e-services marketplace without well-defined and measurable ICT processes. While the management of technologies and application components has been the traditional mainstay of ICT, most ICT service providers are realising that past and even current service delivery has less to do with the technologies, than it does with poorly designed or 'missing' critical ICT processes.

The goal of every ICT service organisation should be alignment with and support of business strategy and objectives. The only way for ICT service organisations to continue to support business needs is by having SM in place. An SM framework provides the focus and objectives for all implemented technologies, for all steps and tasks assigned and for all delegated responsibilities necessary for providing service to the end user. An SM framework also includes the ICT management process that helps the organisation to provide continuously improving service levels for business services from an end-user's perspective. The result of a carefully tooled, well-guided SM framework is improved quality with regard to the level of service provided, which then can be replicated successfully to other business services and business processes. Further, when followed,

SM ensures that the lines of communication between ICT and business stay open as they continue to work together to improve and refine SAs as new business needs and priorities change, changes in the ICT environment occur or the cost of providing established levels of service change.

SM is a process for delivering services that consistently meet customer requirements. An excellent framework for managing ICT costs, SM serves to help firms guarantee, deliver and improve specific application and systems response times for their ICT end users. Knowing where to begin is the challenge in implementing an SM strategy. ICT vendors now offer a variety of point products and solution suites with enough breadth and depth to fit narrowly focused as well as comprehensive SM initiatives.

In order to create and maintain SM, ICT managers need well-defined processes that spring naturally from a disciplined service culture. The clear business rules, proven tools, and methodologies provided by SM help drive ICT service operations toward the elusive goal of alignment with the business. The successful implementation of SM calls for more than buying some software and putting a contract on the desk of the nearest department head. It requires a strategy. This strategy has an organised and flexible plan for introducing SAs and working with them day to day to achieve maximum efficiency and savings. Knowing where to begin with an SM implementation is a challenge, suggesting that mission critical applications are ideal candidates for starting on the SM path.

Upfront planning is the key to the successful implementation of an SM solution. The recognition and prioritisation of business goals are the first steps. The successful implementation of an SM strategy requires the consideration and completion of a number of activities.

1.9.1 Key Components of a Service Management Framework
The presence of an SM implementation framework is of fundamental importance to the success of any subsequent service management initiative. The following five (5) key components are important in an SM framework.

1 Readiness to Provide Services
The provider organisation must be ready to provide services. In order to do this, the provider organisation must have a detailed understanding of their service offerings, with respect to their capacity to offer, manage and sustain services.

2 Eliciting Customer Requirements

The elicitation of customer requirements forms the basis of the relationship between a service provider and a customer, defining the terms of reference. Ensuring that the customer's requirements are identified and acknowledged ensures that there is a basis for the development of a business relationship. This has been widely recognised as a fundamental component of any managed service environment.

3 Understanding, Managing and Documenting Customer Requirements

Management is most straightforward when the requirements are well understood and easily described, and also the means of satisfying them is clear. The identification of requirements is part of the process. These requirements need to be understood by both the customer and the provider. The management of customer requirements includes the verification of the validity and business relevance of each requirement. The exact nature of the customer's requirements and their relationships to business processes must be understood, managed and documented. This documentation is a process that is also undertaken by both the provider and the customer. Requirements might be unclear, might change over time and cannot readily be foreseen. As such the management of customer requirements is not easy, as it requires considerable changes in organisational arrangements, coordination mechanisms, new processes and allocation of responsibilities.

4 Satisfying Customer Requirements

Once the customer's requirements are elicited, understood, managed and documented, the managed service environment can be identified. The next step in the process is to implement the services to satisfy the customer's requirements.

5 Improvements in Services and Business Relationship

The managed services environment should make provision for improvements in services. Initial service levels can be regarded as a benchmark against which improvements can continually be made. If a mutual commitment between customer and provider is made to these improvements, the business relationship is also likely to improve.

For an ICT service provider to be in a position to provide services, certain preparatory activities need to have been completed. These preparatory activities form the platform for any number of service management projects. Without preparing themselves, the ICT service provider organisation will be unable to successfully manage the services they provide.

Once the ICT service provider is in a position to provide services successfully, they can engage any number of customers to whom they can provide services. In other words, once prepared, the ICT service provider can manage services to any variety of customers.

1.10 Conclusion

The management of service levels is a complex, yet necessary evolution in the ICT industry. A characteristic of this evolution after the 'dot com' era are customers that have begun to demand levels of service akin to those provided by utility services. Successful ICT service management can be achieved when key elements of SM are in place and a rigorous implementation framework is adhered to.

There are indeed problems with SM, these problems need to be identified and managed in order to reap the benefits and derive a return on any investment in SM. This chapter has identified this and the following chapter details a framework for SM implementation.

CHAPTER 2

A Framework for the Implementation of Service Management

2.1 Introduction

The framework presented in this chapter recognises that an ICT service provider organisation needs to progress through two phases. The initial phase is characterised by the introspective activities required to place the service provider in a state of service management readiness. This phase is done in the absence of customers. The latter phase is where a customer is engaged and ICT services are being managed.

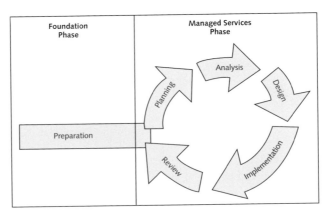

Figure 2.1 *Service Management Framework*

The relevance of an ICT implementation framework is of equal value to service providers as it is to service recipients. Services exist in an environment where there are providers and customers. In many instances, the providers may also be customers. While the perspective of a provider may differ from that of the customer, the success of the service provision depends on the application of the implementation framework. While the service provider needs to complete the activities identified in the foundation phase, the customer needs to seek evidence of the completion of these activities. The managed services phase involves the interaction of both the provider and the customer. The phases and steps identified in the proposed framework below are therefore of relevance to both service providers and customers.

The Foundation Phase comprises all the preparatory activities required for the implementation of SM. These preparatory activities do not result in an environment wherein services are effectively managed. Rather, this initial phase places an organisation in a position of readiness to provide and manage services. This is depicted in Figure 2.1 as a block of preparatory activities positioned before and overlapping into the second phase.

The Managed Services Phase is characterised by a lifecycle of activities that are required when implementing an individual SM project. This cycle is initiated by the Planning step which originates from the Preparatory activities. This cycle continues through Analysis, Design and Implementation steps. The cycle concludes with a Review step that feeds back into the Preparatory activities in order to provide the necessary feedback into the review of the Preparatory activities.

2.2   Phase 1: Foundation

The framework recognises eight key preparatory activities. These activities correspond to the key actions an organisation needs to complete before attempting to provide and manage services. While these activities are interdependent, they are sequential and are of equal priority. The customer can be involved at relevant positions, to enhance the alignment of provider and customer. These eight preparatory activities are:
1. Appoint or nominate Service Management staff
2. Define Service Management scope and objectives
3. Quantify activities, resources, funding and quality criteria
4. Identify risks
5. Raise awareness of Service Management
6. Develop a Service Catalogue and Standard Operating Procedures
7. Identify support tools, especially for SA monitoring
8. Set incident priority levels and escalation paths.

2.2.1 Appoint or Nominate Service Management Staff

This first of the preparatory activities is the appointment or nomination of a service manager and possibly additional service management staff. This signifies the commitment by the organisation to invest in SM, as well as providing an organisational base and leadership for the SM strategy.

The identification of a service manager, who holds a senior position within the organisation, provides a focal point and channel for the management of services. By dedicating resources to SM, the organisation ensures that the development of an SM strategy is thorough and sustainable.

The seniority of the service manager impacts on the credibility of the SM strategy. The more senior the service manager, the more credibility is afforded the SM strategy. Further, the relationship between the head of the organisation's ICT and the service manager is of critical importance. In an in-sourcing environment, the service manager reports to the CIO, whereas in an outsourcing environment, the service manager reports to the executive management structure.

The responsibilities of SM staff include:
- Create and maintain a catalogue of existing services
- Formulate and maintain an appropriate SM structure for the organisation, including:
  - Service Level Agreements structure
  - Operational Level Agreements
  - Third Party Provider / Contract Management relationships
  - Existing Service Improvement Programs
- Manage SAs, OLAs and Service Improvement Processes
- Review service performance against SAs and OLAs
- Produce regular service reports
- Manage service level review process
- Manage quality.

Some of the key skills and competencies include:
- Relationship Management skills
- Project Management skills
- Communication and negotiation skills
- Human Resources management and administrative skills

- Presentation skills
- Understanding of ICT provider services
- Understanding of customer's business.

2.2.2 Define Service Management Scope and Objectives

It is important to ensure alignment of business and ICT strategies. In setting the ICT direction, the management of services form an important part. The identification of a strategic direction, that aligns ICT with the business, enables the business to achieve improved service delivery and provide the flexibility to cope with change. In order to achieve this, policies and standards are required for consistent management of ICT. These encapsulate the vision, scope and objectives of the SM strategy.

In order to define the scope and objectives of an SM strategy, the following key features need to be considered:
- The flexibility to exploit opportunities, as well as to respond to external change
- A mechanism for accountability
- A framework for managing risk
- A mechanism for translating ICT developments into new business opportunities.

In order to develop the scope and objectives, the following activities need to be completed:
- Analysis of business needs and how ICT can support their attainment
- Establishing of a policy of risk management
- Establishing an ICT strategy that integrates the business strategy and raises awareness of the contribution of ICT towards the business outcomes
- Recognition of future developments and business opportunities.

2.2.3 Quantify Activities, Resources, Funding and Quality Criteria

Once the scope and objectives of the SM program have been identified, the necessary activities, resources, funding and quality criteria need to be quantified. These four activities are closely related and each impacts on the other three. For example, if the quality criteria increase, a corresponding increase is required in the funding, this then impacts on the allocation of resources leading to a refinement of the activities.

The development of job descriptions and work break down structures, along with the allocation of portfolios are the key components in quantifying activities.

Allocating and mapping resources to these activities is an important consideration. Ensuring that the appropriate skill sets are properly coupled to the task requirements impacts on the success of the initiative.

Funding is often problematic. These problems are two fold. Primarily, the sourcing of funding is difficult. This is compounded in an environment where there is limited buy-in from executive management. Secondarily, creating a balance between activities, resources and quality, within a financially controlled environment requires skilled planning. Compromise on any of these activities to save costs can diminish the effectiveness of an SM program.

The quality criteria identified in an SM initiative requires in-depth analysis of the business processes and requirements. In benchmarking network and device uptime, as well as stipulating response times requires careful consideration of the impact these have on the business as a whole. Further, the priority of incidents needs to be considered before they can be quantified in terms of up-time and response time.

2.2.4 Identify Risks

The organisation derives added value from a continued service improvement program. A business case for implementing SM recognises the projected costs and revenue. In reality, the costs are easy to describe and manage as they refer to people, time, tools, hardware and software. However, the improvements in revenue and or savings as a direct result of the improvements in service levels are more difficult to quantify.

The development of a business case requires a detailed understanding of the business need and scope before the change process can be undertaken. The business case should provide senior management with sufficient information to enable them to make decisions. These decisions consider the business needs and priorities of any improvement projects, and help assure that the project is justified in terms of acceptable costs, quantified benefits and indented risks.

A structured approach to risk management is an important part of the preparatory SM activities. Risk management occurs once risks have been identified and analyzed. In identifying risks, the following three risk areas need to be considered:
- The business vision
- The existing business processes
- The environment and business constraints.

The risks associated with a continued service improvement program can be classified into three categories:

- **Conceptual** - relating to the scope of the continued service improvement process
- **Technical** - relating to the processes and procedures adopted by the organisation
- **Resource** - covering the skills and competencies necessary to deliver a successful change and improvement in service management.

2.2.5 Raise Awareness of Service Management

Although the definition of the SM scope and objectives are helpful tools and guide, the true benefits are only seen when these are communicated to all the associated stakeholders. Typically the stakeholder interest stems from the fact that they have invested time, energy, attention, money and resources with the expectation of a return on their investment.

A sense of urgency ('what if we do nothing?') and the vision ('what is in it for me?') should form the basis of all communication to the stakeholders. Aim these messages at motivating, inspiring and creating the necessary energy, commitment and buy-in.

Use all the available communication channels. Examples of these include the organisation's newsletters, intranet, posters, meetings and seminars. Aim the communication at the specific needs of each target group.

2.2.6 Develop a Service Catalogue and Standard Operating Procedures

Service Management is a process that defines, negotiates, monitors, reports, and controls customer-specific service levels within predefined standard service parameters. It also generates customer-specific services if the SA requires it. A Service Catalogue is where all this information is contained in one place for service documentation, coordination, maintenance, and referral.

A Service Catalogue focuses specifically on documenting and articulating the ICT services provided by the service provider. Typically it also contains the optional service levels that are usually detailed in an SA. Such a catalogue lists all of the services being provided, a summary of their characteristics and details of the customer as well as the catalogue maintainer.

For a comprehensive model for the development of a Service Catalogue we refer to Chapter 3.

Standard Operating Procedures (SOPs) are contained in a document that defines each and every business activity and process. This document describes not only what the organisation does, but how it does it. Included in this document are the following:

- The definitions of the various business units
- The key operating procedures for each unit
- The human resource and industrial relation rules and procedures
- The activities of employee and business administration, including record keeping and reporting
- The relevant job descriptions.

It has become imperative to put company procedures down on paper. Compliance to quality standards such as ISO 9000 and ISO/IEC 20000 requires companies to document their operating procedures. The process of documenting SOPs is something that must be planned before being attempted.

Unlike other forms of writing, SOPs are written from a technical and managerial perspective. This means they must be:

- **Clear and concise** - getting directly to the point: SOPs should be communicated in the fewest possible words, phrases, and paragraphs
- **Complete** - containing all the necessary information to perform the procedure
- **Objective** - containing facts, not opinions
- **Coherent -** showing a logical thought process and sequentially listing all steps necessary to complete the procedure.

SOPs can serve as benchmarks for performance reviews, training aids, or in the case of quality standards, a starting point for improvement.

You will find the following tips helpful when writing standard operating procedures:

- Always have a specific reader in mind. You should know the type of person who will be reading the procedure. When you know the level of experience of the reader, you can tailor the writing accordingly.
- Before starting to write, decide the exact purpose of the procedure. Once you have decided the exact purpose of the procedure, make sure everything you write contributes to that purpose.
- Start with an introductory paragraph that briefly describes the procedure. This is followed by a complete description of the procedure, using the most appropriate writing technique (paragraphs, bullet points, and so on) to communicate key aspects of the procedure. Finally, a concluding paragraph should be written that summarises the main points covered.

- Make an outline of the procedure prior to writing. The purpose of an outline is to establish an orderly relationship between groups of activities. An outline provides a framework for any documentation. When writing an outline:
  - Make a list of topics to be covered. The order is not important; just don't omit anything that you feel is appropriate to the topic.
  - Decide on major groups. Groups may include introduction, responsibilities, safety issues, operating characteristics, background information, and summary.
  - Insert the topics under the appropriate major group.
- Write a rough draft. Keep in mind that a good procedure is rarely achieved on the first draft. Write rapidly, ignoring spelling, punctuation, and grammar. Write as you talk so you can maintain a train of thought. Write the draft with the outline in front of you to serve as a guide.
- Revise the draft. Wait 24 hours before making revisions. Revising too soon is less effective because the writer often sees not what is on the paper, but what was meant. Examine what the sentences say, and then be willing to rewrite every part of the procedure.
- Write the final draft, incorporating all of the latest revisions.
- Watch for your own boredom. If you become bored as you are writing, there is a good chance your readers will also.

In addition to the preceding tips on writing SOPs, there are pitfalls to avoid, including:
- Vague, meaningless words
- Excessive words to describe an activity
- Long, complicated sentences or paragraphs
- Acronyms, abbreviations, slang, symbols, or other shortcuts of expression that are not clearly defined for the reader
- Repeating the same points too often
- Assuming that conclusions are obvious to the reader.

2.2.7 Identify Support Tools, Especially for SA Monitoring

It is important to identify the appropriate tools for monitoring service levels. A number of factors need to be considered when assessing these tools.

Often a range of tools is available throughout the organisational departments. These tools need to be identified and analyzed. More often than not:
- There is little integration or sharing of data between these tools.
- Tools that support specific processes do not support the functional level required by the SM initiative.

- Data structures and handling cannot be tailored to record attributes and data to support work flows.

It is important to define specific requirements in terms of technology-enabled processes requiring improvement, for example:
- Which processes and functionality can be effectively supported
- Which processes are required and what functionality is demanded for each process
- What data has to be captured to carry out and report upon process performance effectively?
- What level of process integration is required in the tool support – the ability to link incidents to problems?

Once this information has been gathered and the existing tool support is analyzed, a clearer picture emerges about:
- Whether or not any of the existing tools meet requirements
- Whether the existing data needs to migrate to a new tool, or if it is necessary to implement a new integrated Service Management tool
- Where the current skills and expertise in using and configuring tools exist.

Consideration must be given to the exact requirements for the tool. The following are some practical guidelines for selecting an SM tool:
- The tool must support the process; the process must not be modified to fit the tool.
- Where possible, it is better to purchase a fully integrated tool to underpin as many of the SM processes as possible.
- The tool must support access rights flexible.
- Initial consideration must include the hardware and software operating platform for compatibility with the tool.
- Negotiate with the selected vendors and include on site demonstrations and reference sites to visit.
- Assess the management reports generated by the tool.
- Assess the training needs of the organisation in order to implement the tool as well as the support offered by the vendor.
- Ensure that the tool interfaces with other tools and telephony.
- Describe the manual interfaces where the tool does not support all process activities.

2.2.8   Set Incident Priority Levels and Escalation Paths

The priority of an incident is primarily determined by the *impact* on the business and the *urgency* with which a resolution or work-around is needed. Targets for resolving incidents or handling requests are generally embodied in an SLA within the SA. In practice, resolution targets for incidents are often related to categories.

Incident classification is the process of identifying the reason(s) for the incident and hence the corresponding resolution action(s). Many incidents are regularly experienced and the appropriate resolution actions are well known. This is not always the case, however, and a procedure for matching incident classification data against that for problems and known errors is necessary. Successful matching gives access to proven resolution actions, which should require no further investigation effort.

In order to classify incidents, the following inputs are required:
- Recorded details of incidents
- Configuration details from the Change Management Database and the Configuration Management Database
- Response from incident matched against problems and known errors.

Incident records raised in the input phase are now analyzed to discover the reason for the incident. The incident should also be classified, the process step on which further resolution actions are based.

Once the inputs have been gathered, the following processes and actions need to be performed:
- Classify incidents
- Matching against known errors and problems
- Informing problem management of the existence of new problems and of unmatched or multiple incidents
- Assigning impact and urgency – defining priority
- Assessing related configuration details
- Providing initial support (access incident and find a quick resolution)
- Closing the incident or routing to a specialist support group and informing the user(s).

The outputs of the classification process are:
- Incident resolution (optional)
- Updated incident details

- Work-arounds for incidents (optional), or incident routed to second or third line support.

2.3   Phase 2: Managed Services

Once the SM foundations have been laid, any number of service management projects can be initiated. The framework identifies five key steps for the managing of services. While these steps detail a chronological path for an SM implementation, they provide flexibility of movement in both directions.

The Managed Services Phase begins with linking the Foundation Phase to the Planning step. The Planning step leads into the Analysis, which is followed, in chronological order, by Design, Implementation and Review steps.

2.3.1   Planning

Three planning activities occur in the implementation of an SM project. Firstly, identify, with the customer, a broad understanding of the required services. Secondly, members of the SM team are identified. Once the SM project has been initiated, the final step is to raise awareness of it.

Meet with Customer
Once the capacity to manage services has been established, the service provider can approach potential customers who require those services. The objective of this initial meeting is to establish the link between what managed services the provider is able and willing to provide and those that the customer requires. If the managed services on offer match those required, the SM project can proceed.

Establish SM Project Team
When the managed services on offer map to those that are required, the stakeholders provide human resources to the SM project. It is advisable for the project team to be made up of resources from both the customer and the provider's organisations. This team needs to complete the following activities:

- **Assign roles and responsibilities** - Each team member must have an identifiable and agreed role with associated responsibilities. This will provide focus to each team member as well as providing the links between people, as 'who does what' is documented and communicated between team members. The structure of the team and the associated relationships between its members provides the transparency of where responsibilities lie.

- **Prepare work flows / Gantt chart** - The second task of the SM project team is to detail the proposed activities against time, taking consideration of the associations and dependencies that exist between tasks.

Raise Awareness of SM Project

Once the customer and the provider have agreed to enter into a service relationship, and have settled on the structure and makeup of a project team, they need to raise awareness of the SM project. This can be done in a number of ways. It is advisable to enlist the support and help of the marketing and/or communication departments of either or both the parties. It is important to publicise the 'why', 'when' and 'how' of the proposed SM project. This improvement in the profile of the project assists in ensuring the support and buy-in of all parties affected by the resulting changes. It also helps to improve employee moral as more employees are made aware of the pending improved management of services.

2.3.2 Analysis

When all the planning activities are complete, the SM project team can focus on providing a managed services solution. An in-depth analysis of the customer's business processes and their existing services are a starting point to provide a picture of the customer's current situation. When this picture is complete, the appropriate services that support the customer's business processes can be identified and catalogued to map the managed services solution.

Identify Customer's Business Processes

Analysis of the customer's operating procedures and businesses processes is a critical part of any SM project. The identification and understanding of how the customer conducts their business is of pivotal importance as the future of the SM project is guided by this. Any managed service environment is worthless, if the services do not assist or complement these business processes.

Review Customer's Existing Services

Unless the project is green fields in nature, or the customer requires a new service, it is probable that services are already in place. These existing services need to be reviewed and assessed in light of the identified business processes, the customer's requirements and the provider's capacity to provide them. In a best case scenario, there may already be an existing fit between the business processes and the managed services. Alternatively, there may be a requirement for an adaptation of the managed services. In a worst case scenario, the customer's managed services may need to be completely overhauled.

A special situation occurs when (new) services are retrieved from an existing outsourcing partner. In that case, specific attention has to be given to contractual issues in the transition.

Identify the Services to Support those Business Processes
Once the business processes and the service environment have been identified and reviewed, the appropriate managed services need to be mapped to support the business processes.

Develop a Blueprint of the customer's Service Requirements
The conclusion of the analysis step is the development of a blueprint of the customer's service requirements. The successful mapping of managed services to business processes is the result of the analysis step. Poorly executed analysis increases the probability of failure in the SM project. This situation may arise when the service provider has failed to understand the customer's business processes and/or requirements. Additional factors that could contribute to the failure of an SM project are an over-commitment by the provider to manage services beyond its capacity.

A review of this blueprint by all stakeholders and possibly an independent authority could assist in the identification of these potential pitfalls.

2.3.3 Design
With the blueprint of the customer's service requirements as a reference tool, the managed services solution can be designed. The primary activity in this step is the negotiation and development of an SA.

For a comprehensive model for the development of Service Agreements, refer to Chapter 4.

2.3.4 Implementation
Once an SA has been negotiated and created, it needs to be implemented. The implementation step in this framework is characterised by the deployment of the SA. If the Foundation phase and the previous steps in the Managed Services phase have been accurately completed, the deployment of the SA will be routine. It is a common error for an SM project to begin by attempting to implement an SA.

Deploy SA
With the comprehensive design of the SA, the deployment thereof is routine. The skills of the implementation team are technical and their actions are governed by the

developed document. A well structured SA that has been developed in accordance with this framework is easier to implement than one developed in parallel with the implementation of a managed services environment.

Real-time Monitoring of Service Levels

Service managers must see to it that the required service levels are monitored. For services to be effectively managed, they need to be monitored in real-time. A myriad of tools monitor all aspects of an ICT environment. These tools provide service managers with accurate and current information regarding the state of all devices and processes operating across a variety of mediums.

Not only does real-time monitoring provide information on the current status across a broad spectrum of hardware and software devices and programs, it assists in the proactive management of services. Problems can be avoided if early warning signals are identified and attended to.

Service Level Reporting

Service levels in a managed environment must be referenced against those stipulated in the SA. Performance over a specified time can be assessed against the criteria set out in the SA. Detailed reporting should be done monthly and summarised annually. When reporting, it is good to accommodate the 4 W's. What happened, what caused it, what harm was done and what has been done to avoid it happening again in the future. This reporting provides an opportunity for the provider and customer to identify areas of strengths and weaknesses as well as provide a platform for the flexibility identified in the eight SA development principles discussed in Chapter 4.

2.3.5   Review

A managed services environment is dynamic. Technology is constantly changing and the requirements of the customer are also subject to change. These changes impact on the ability to provide and manage services. Review comprises three key activities:

Review Service Levels

There is no room for complacency with respect to service levels. These need to be continually reviewed in line with business requirements and advances in technology. The monthly reporting interaction between the customer and provider provides a platform for the initial review of service levels. The annual summary report is an additional interaction between customer and provider to review services.

Establish Priorities and Plan for Change
Due to the dynamic nature of the ICT environment, change is inevitable. Priorities are also subject to change. The recognition of this is important. Planning for this is therefore of paramount importance if the managed services environment is to be flexible and sustainable to the benefit of all stakeholders.

Fine Tune or Reengineer Business Processes and/or Services
In reviewing service levels and embracing change, the organisation accepts that business processes and services are dynamic and are subject to change. Improvements in the way we do things, as well as improvements in the technology that assists us, occur regularly. As a result, there is a continued need to refine both the business processes and the managed services that support them.

The review step of the Managed Services Phase provides a link back into the Foundation Phase. This allows for the revision of the preparatory activities to make necessary adjustments in light of the lessons learnt in an SM project.

2.4   Conclusion

The strength of this framework is the recognition of, and the emphasis on, the preparatory activities. A criticism of some of the approaches towards SM has been the failure to identify and clarify the foundational activities necessary before embarking on a service management initiative.

CHAPTER 3

A Model for the Development of a Service Catalogue

3.1 Introduction

The goal of an ICT Service Catalogue is to standardise, integrate and contain all the services that are provided by an ICT services provider. This is accomplished through a single repository from which ICT can serve the needs of all customers and proactively manage the portfolio of ICT services. This chapter explores a model of ICT Service Catalogue development, from the initial planning through the implementation and on to ongoing maintenance (see Figure 3.1).

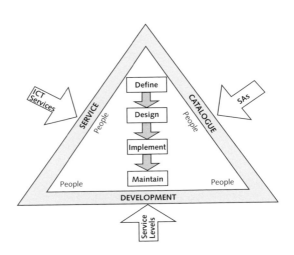

Figure 3.1 *A Model for Service Catalogue Development*

There are three key components involved in the development of a Service Catalogue:
- ICT Services
- SAs
- Service Levels.

3.2   Components of the ICT Service Catalogue

The model comprises three components for the development of a Service Catalogue.

3.2.1   ICT Services

A major component of SM is the definition of ICT services within a Service Catalogue. It is from this definition that SAs are negotiated with the customer. It is imperative that services, including those that are provided to a customer, or consumed internally within ICT, or whether delivered internally or via an external service provider or supplier, be defined in the catalogue.

3.2.2   Service Agreements

Once the services have been established, performance indicators, including availability and reliability, should be considered. Using a draft SA, while developing the Service Catalogue, helps provide better understanding of the customer's business. This will have a knock-on effect in improving the relationship between provider and customer.

3.2.3   Service Levels

The levels of services are an important issue in all Service Catalogues. It cannot be stressed enough that Service Catalogues must contain measurable metrics that adequately represent the services involved so that the services can be provided at the appropriate service levels.

3.3   Service Catalogue Development

When developing a Service Catalogue, the many different groups of people have vested interests that need to be considered. The following groups of people should be considered: the service provider, the customer, users, service managers and service teams. All these groups need to be accommodated if the resulting Service Catalogue is to accurately document the desired service provision.

There are four steps in Service Catalogue development:
- Define
- Design
- Implement
- Maintain.

3.3.1 Define the Service Catalogue

In order to improve something, it must first be defined. The first step in the creation of an ICT Service Catalogue is the definition and development of a comprehensive list of ICT services and systems that the ICT organisation provides to its customer base. Once the services have been defined, Service Level Objectives (SLOs) can be determined. Each service should be linked to a desired business goal or outcome. Good examples include understanding the true, total costs of delivering ICT services and, defining in detail a specific set of services that are candidates for outsourcing. Over time, these objectives should be deepened in breadth, scope, and detail.

3.3.2 Design the Service Catalogue

A Service Catalogue can appear in many different formats, such as word documents, spreadsheets, web pages. To make a Service Catalogue worthwhile within an ICT organisation, it should be designed to include all information needed to support initiatives such as:
- Service Management
- Change Management
- Service Information
- Ownership
- Support
- Authority
- Financial Information.

The following service information and metrics must also be included:
- Service Name
- Service Description
- Service Levels
- Key Business Users
- Key Support areas
- Planned Maintenance
- Service Reporting.

The catalogue should be designed to work with, or act as input to an SA, which serves as an underpinning for the standardisation of definitions and terminology. In some cases, SAs may be replaced with a Service Catalogue that defines the same information. The Service Catalogue should be integrated with the SAs and the SLOs, ensuring that it has a business and customer service focus. Finally, the look and feel of the Service Catalogue should be simple, straightforward, intuitive and accessible.

3.3.3   Implement the Service Catalogue

The Service Catalogue is most effective when implemented jointly between the ICT service provider and the customer as the two groups cooperate. The following should be considered when implementing a Service Catalogue:

- Start with putting together a list of proposed services and estimated service levels.
- Call for an informal meeting with business stakeholders. This is truly the first step in the way the customer will view ICT services, and as such, ICT has to be prepared for the change.
- Validate the proposed list of ICT services.
- Confirm the SAs.
- Establish how compliance to these contracts will be measured and reported to the business.
- Assign and train service managers (and associated resources if necessary) whose primary role and responsibility will be to support SM organisation-wide.
- Consider off-the-shelf software and the associated hardware initially for practical reasons of maintenance, support, and resource requirements.
- Roll out the complete Service Catalogue and verify it with the customer community.
- Assign the responsibility of maintaining and enhancing the Service Catalogue.
- Fully develop the other interrelated areas of ITSM as needed, that is, Change Management, Application Management and Problem Management. This helps ensure that an optimised maturity level is attained as uniformly as possible.

Service providers should strive to create an actionable ICT Service Catalogue that:

- Defines services in the language that customers will understand
- Is available to all staff members
- Can be used as a source to copy from, when placing a service order
- Provides performance management data for ICT services.

3.3.4   Maintain the Service Catalogue

When slow economic conditions prevail, many customers try to find ways to reduce the expenses associated with delivering internal services without compromising quality. The definition of Service Catalogue is a necessary first step; however, it is evident that automation of a Systems Design and Management (SDM) tool can deliver added savings and provide service consistency for both internal service organisations and external service providers. Although Service Catalogues can be created using something as simple as spreadsheets or word processors, using an SDM system facilitates quicker achievement of benefits cross the full set of service delivery tasks than those that only use the catalogue as an information store.

3.4 Conclusion

A Service Catalogue places the service provider in a position to effectively provide and manage services. The ability to know exactly what you are capable of doing provides a solid foundation to attract customers. A Service Catalogue makes ICT services tangible for the business so it can better weigh its cost-quality options before signing on (and paying for) ICT services. The importance and value of a comprehensive Service Catalogue can not be underestimated.

CHAPTER 4

A Model for the Negotiation and Development of Service Agreements

4.1 Introduction

The successful development of an SA is vital to the continuing relationship between a customer and a service provider. An SA documents the terms of the business relationship between the stakeholders. It is thus important that the SA development process involves all the stakeholders that will be affected by the intended service provision. The SA needs to document exactly what services will be provided and at what levels, along with procedures for dealing with service issues should they arise. SAs are usually in effect for between three and five years, so the original authors of the SA may not be available if a problem arises. The document needs to be detailed enough to allow any new stakeholder to effectively participate in the relationship.

The model for the development of an SA comprises two phases.
1. The **first phase** details the various complex forces that have a bearing on the development process. Each force has a sphere of influence that can have a bearing on the entire process or just a small part of it. The Development Team (DT) must continuously take these forces into account during the development process. These are depicted by the circles around the outer sphere of Figure 4.1.
2. The **second phase** is represented as a set of steps that the Negotiation Team must physically perform. The steps are: Define; Monitor and Agree; Document; and Review and Optimise. The four-step process is repeated for each Service Level Agreement (SLA). This is depicted by the set of steps in the centre of Figure 4.1.

4.2 The Development Team

The Preparation development principle discusses the need to establish a group of individuals who are charged with the development of the SA. This group is known as the Development Team (DT). This team should be comprised of between three to five members. These members should come from finance, legal, sales and technical divisions. Preference should be given to people with experience in developing SAs.

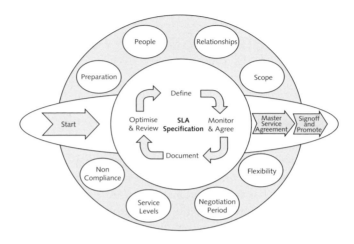

Figure 4.1 *Model for Service Agreement Development*

A customer should also be included in the DT. The formation of the team must be formally announced to all stakeholders, as everybody in the organisation(s) are involved and affected by the process.

4.3   Development Principles

The model comprises eight development principles that have a bearing on the SA development. The DT must bear these in mind at every stage of the SA specification. These are: The Negotiation Period; Preparation; People; Relationships; Scope; Service Levels; Non Compliance; and Flexibility.

4.3.1   The Negotiation Period

One of the most important aspects of the SA development process is the length of time allocated to the process. It is not conducive to successful negotiations to specify a time limit for those negotiations. An SA is an excellent tool for helping service providers and their customers improve communications, manage expectations, clarify responsibilities, and build the foundation for a mutually beneficial relationship. Many factors can influence the duration of the effort, such as:

- **The service environment** - The more services covered by an SA, and the more complex these services, the longer it takes the two parties to discuss, negotiate and document the conditions of service delivery.
- **The proximity of the parties** - Face-to-face negotiation is crucial in establishing an SA. However, if travel is needed to enable this face-to-face contact, it can add significantly to the elapsed time.
- **The span of impact of the SA** - Establishing an SA between two parties in a home office generally takes less time than establishing an SA that spans regional, national or international boundaries.
- **The relationship between the parties** - When the relationship is characterised by trust and respect, the effort proceeds much more quickly than when it is marred by distrust and dissatisfaction. In the latter situation, additional steps may be needed to begin to repair the relationship before undertaking the more formal SA process.
- **The availability of a model** - The first SA in an organisation usually takes the longest time to construct. Once it is completed and in operation, however, both the document and the process can serve as a model for subsequent SAs. If the first SA is successful, later ones usually proceed much more rapidly.
- **Prior SA experience** - The most expeditious SA efforts are those led by SA developers who have had prior successful experience establishing an SA. Conversely, if prior experience is lacking or failed to result in an effective SA, the development process often hobbles along.
- **The origination of services to be delivered** - Quantity, quality and costs may differ a lot depending on where the services are being originated. Outsourced services can be more standard and easily bought in and shorten the negotiation period whereas the in-house deliverance is more flexible towards business interpretation and may lengthen the implementation period. There are several pros and contras for every situation.

Too short

A misconception about SAs regularly encountered is that they can be created quickly. Some stakeholders begin under orders from management to complete the negotiations the following week. Management mandates notwithstanding, participants soon understand the impossibility of this task, and face the challenges of helping their management achieve this same understanding.

Developing an SA in a week or even a month is both difficult and inadvisable. It is difficult because of the extensive workload involved in such tasks as negotiating service standards, establishing tracking mechanisms, preparing supporting procedures, gaining approvals and generating buy-in. And it is inadvisable because the process is designed to help the two parties build the foundation for a strong, successful, long-term relationship. To rush this process is to sabotage the entire effort.

Too long

Too long refers not to a specific time period, but to an effort that has stalled and is making no progress. One major contributor to a stalled effort is a lack of familiarity with the process of establishing an SA. A second major reason that the effort often stalls, is that one or both parties fail to bring a serious commitment to the effort. When management refuses to allocate staff to establish the SA, or the effort is given a low priority, or one or both parties are unwilling to negotiate in good faith, progress becomes impossible.

Just right

Establishing an SA is typically a many-month process of information-gathering, analyzing, documenting, educating, negotiating, and consensus-building. Three to six months is a reasonable amount of time. When circumstances are optimal, three months is realistic, and sometimes even less. At the other extreme, if the situation is complex, six months may not be enough. However, if significant progress has not been made within six months, it is time to stop the effort and examine why.

4.3.2   Preparation

The first action that must be taken when developing an SA is to formally announce the DT. The new DT must then set ground rules for working together. This is done to avoid any unnecessary ill feeling developing later in the negotiation. The DT must delegate major areas of responsibility, namely communications, and document collation. Although these invariably change throughout the negotiation period, it helps to set a starting point.

The DT now needs to develop a template SA. This serves as an outline for the negotiations and closely resembles a table of contents. Whilst developing this document, the DT needs to specify formatting styles such as font styles, structural layout and specific terms/abbreviations for the document and detail these decisions in the SA.

A key factor in the success of the negotiations is identifying the human resource requirement. The set of skills and experience team members bring to the project should be appropriate to that particular SA development. Clearly identifying project stakeholders early in the process allows the sponsor and project manager to see the 'landscape' of the organisations and individuals they must involve in order to make the project successful.

A list of characteristics of these stakeholders facilitates:

- Establishing the most appropriate project sponsorship based on power, structure, and influence.
- Understanding what stakeholders must contribute (resources, advocacy) to the project.
- Selecting project participants in the early phases, as well as throughout the project.

Establishing ground rules for working together is a critical, but often overlooked, step. The SA developers (those assigned to negotiate the SA) focus not on the SA, but on the process by which they will work together to create the SA. Issues to be discussed include the division of responsibility for development tasks, scheduling issues and constraints, and concerns regarding potential impediments. In addition, the developers can benefit greatly by discussing their communication styles and preferences. By identifying similarities and differences at the start of the negotiation period, they will be in an excellent position to minimise conflict.

It is important to involve the customer from the outset of the SA development process, but rather than going along with a blank sheet to commence with, it may be better to use a template as a starting point for more detailed and in-depth discussion. An SA template is a skeleton document that contains not much more than the headings of the intended document and some of the standard contractual elements. An SA template is very different to a standard SA. In an attempt to speedup negotiations, service providers frequently have a standard SA that generally covers their services and is usually not customised for each customer.

The degree to which a standard SA can be used in SA negotiations depends entirely on the complexity of the SA and the previous SA experience of the Development Team. If an SA is for a single service that is mass produced, like a cellular telephone contract, then there is no point in conducting active negotiations over a three month period with each user. Just offer a small range of standard 'packages' for the customer to choose from. This way, the customer can select a package that closely resembles their requirements. However, if an SA covers an extensive service provision for a multinational conglomerate, it is unlikely that a generic SA exists that covers the service provision required. Thus, a far more intensive negotiation needs to take place and an SA template and Service Catalogue can be used.

When comparing several SAs within a single ICT organisation, it is frequently found that there are many kinds of formats, styles, layouts, and terms being used. These are situations that should be avoided, especially when trying to minimising downtime of critical applications to prevent loss of business. A standard template is recommended when defining SAs, and that the customer must insist that the service provider uses their templates and definitions.

Experience is also an aspect that needs careful consideration. An expert in the development of SAs will know which aspects will require negotiation and consensus and which aspects are simply industry standards.

4.3.3 People

The SA defines the roles of both the customer and the service provider. As a result, the customer understands exactly what they are expected to do. The service provider is also agreeing on what needs to be done on the customer's behalf. It is critical to involve all customer stakeholders who will be responsible for ensuring SA compliance in the SA development process.

There are three main types of people involved in the creation of an SA. They are: the customer, the service provider, and the user. When developing and managing the SA the customer organisation interfaces with the service provider in two distinct ways:

1. The customer party, purchaser of the service, is responsible for developing the SA with the service provider team.
2. The customer and service provider must agree to terms of the SA and the customer is responsible for using the service according to the SA.

The users of the service discuss day-to-day operational issues with the service provider and give important feedback to the service team on the performance of the service and service improvement recommendations. It is imperative to identify, at the outset of an SA development project, those who will play these major roles in the organisation.

In order for the SA to document these aspects properly, all individuals involved in the eventual delivery of these services need to be involved in the development process. The following stakeholders should always be involved in the negotiations to varying degrees:

- **Service provider** - Provides the range of services to one or more organisations.
- **Customer** - The buyer of the service. The customer will buy services from the service provider in response to user's needs.
- **User** - The one who uses all or some of the services described in the SA.
- **Service Manager** - The person in the customer organisation responsible for ensuring the availability of all services to the user according to the agreed SA and any related contracts. Typically, the service manager will be responsible for a related group of

services and will run several service teams. Service managers should have a good understanding of the business and how it uses the services.

- **Service Team** - The group responsible for defining all service deliverables and establishing measures for these deliverables. One person may be a member of several service teams. The team often comprises the supplier, the customer and the user staff (from divisions including Sales and Marketing, Finance, and ICT)
- **Finance Manager** - The primary reason for entering into an SA is frequently financial. The financial manager can also lend the process considerable credibility.
- **Legal Advisors** - A legal adviser with experience in outsourcing contracts is able to provide valuable input into the issues that need to be addressed, such as the schedules that need to be prepared, and the various options available for structuring the relationship for example.

Whatever approach to development is taken it is important at a very early stage to form a project team which should prepare a project plan which includes all the activities that need to be undertaken to reach a successful sign-off of the SA. Once the team has briefed itself on the range of issues that need to be addressed, it is then possible for subject matter experts to commence preparation of the relevant parts of the Agreement. It is essential, however, that the whole team work together to put the SA together.

Because the organisation that is about to embark on a service sourcing project has probably never been involved in one of these transactions before, it is essential that it assesses at an early stage the sort of advice and assistance that is needed to successfully complete the transaction. One of the mistakes that many organisations make is assuming that since they have been involved in the provision of the service, that they will know how to draw-up the documentation which describes the services to be provided and the levels at which these are to be provided. Experience suggests, however, that it is often extremely difficult for these people to carry out this task and it is usually advisable to seek assistance from a person who has experience in preparing such documentation. Consultants could be approached to assist in this regard.

In complex software licensing and software development projects, as well as outsourcing arrangements, the transaction documents consist initially of a master agreement and a series of schedules, project plans, and SLAs. Later, the parties will enter into various statements of works and amendments to govern new work. Litigations arising from these agreements are often fact intensive and involve the definition of the parties' obligations, software functionality, the exact scope of outsource services, and whether performance justified payment and at what price. These issues are governed in many cases by service level schedules, statements of works, and other technical documents. Because of the litigation impact of these documents, there is a danger in having them drafted solely by technical personnel. For this reason, it is important that lawyers are involved in the drafting of these documents. It is important that the lawyers understand the technical terminology or work closely with experts who do.

Unless the team works together the SA is unlikely to be coherent, workable or effectively able to manage the provision of the services from the service provider.

4.3.4 Relationships
Well structured SAs are recognised as an important step in managing the expectations between service providers and the customers. Although it takes effort to both implement and maintain, an SA is in the best interest of both the service provider and the customer. By developing a set of mutually agreed-upon service characteristics, customers know which services and response times are provided. They also know at what baseline costs these services are provided. The service provider can show that it is providing timely services to corporate management and department users in language that is understandable to them. An SA provides a framework for getting additional ICT resources when adding applications or improving existing services.

In an SA, both the customer and the service provider will pursue their own goals while being concerned about their own lack of complete project control and wary of opportunistic behaviour by their partner. These problems may be reduced somewhat through cautious vendor selection and appropriate structures, but they also require development of trust between the participants. It is especially seen in outsourcing relationships that because participants from both sides often lack prior business relationships with one another and take a short-term, project-centred view.

Moreover, trust can be difficult to develop in outsourcing projects, which are often governed through structural mechanisms, including deliverables, penalty clauses, and reporting arrangements.

There are three different kinds of trust:
1. **Competence Trust** - A trusts B to do a good job because A assumes that B has the required knowledge and skills.
2. **Ethical Trust** - A trusts B because A assumes that B will behave according to A's expectations and will take care of A's interest.
3. **Emotional Trust** - A trusts B because A likes B.

These types of trust do not just comprise different levels or strengths of trust, but are based on different sources: on proof (competence trust), expectation, experience, culture and observation (ethical trust) or on feelings and preferences (emotional trust). They exist and develop relatively independently from each other. Consequently, the level of trust one party displays is not just one-dimensional, but three-dimensional - the combination of three levels different types of trust. Furthermore, trust is dynamic - it depends on the situation, the other party and changes over the course of the relationship.

Distrust has a negative impact on performance, whereas trust improves performance. Distrust can lead to finger pointing, as each organisation focuses on its own interests, seeking to identify how the other organisation may have hurt the project. In contrast, trust characterises successful projects. Mutual trust encourages participants to work together rather than seek ways to deflect blame.

An SA should not be considered merely as a formal contract between financial and legal representatives of a customer and a service provider. This restricts the practical operational value of an SA considerably. Consensus building is one of the major aspects of SA specification and is covered by:

- Content agreement (both services and service levels)
- Conflict prevention (service provider promises versus customer expectations)
- Distinction between service processes (of a service provider) and the business process (in a company)
- Expectation management (expectations are not stable, expectations change).

Service levels are often not met because of the lack of communication between service providers, customers and users with reference to the service levels. Therefore, good communication is necessary for reaching consensus concerning which items to include in the service levels, setting end-user expectations, developing trust and developing the procedures governing how these items are reported.

Over time, customers start to expect more, in terms of speed, functionality, and availability. This is compounded by the increased usage and demand on the underlying infrastructure. There is potential for growth in the number of users accessing systems, additional applications being loaded on servers, and new technology being added to the service provision mixture, all of which taxes infrastructure performance. Good SAs help to avoid this phenomenon by involving all parties in active ongoing negotiations about service levels and what it takes to achieve them. SAs should be revisited periodically to refresh everyone's memory. If service levels decrease, the service provider can point to changes in these circumstances as clear reasons why, and both parties can go back to the table to renegotiate the agreement. In this kind of situation a healthy trusting relationship is needed between the two parties in order for a consensus to be reached.

The service provider and business units must develop SA's in partnership. An SA should outline what business users can expect in terms of system response, quantities of work processed, system availability and system reliability. An SA should also detail the measurement procedures to collect the service-level data and any limitations to the agreed-upon service provisions. It is critical to describe the services in terms that business users understand.

The success of the relationship between the service provider and the customer depends on essential components including:
- A clear understanding of the service provider's capacity to provide a service
- A similar understanding of the customer's expectations of this service
- An appreciation of the limitation of each
- An agreement that addresses all of these
- Ongoing management of the relationship based on that agreement.

The various sources of information used for this section believe that relationship building is of prime importance. Together with the formal contract, a spirit of cooperation needs to be developed, that will enhance the relationship and maintain it during times of difficulty.

4.3.5 Scope

Service Sourcing Decisions

The most important part of every SA is the description of the services that are to be provided by the service provider. This is one of the most difficult tasks encountered when preparing the SA. It is often the case in an organisation that the group (in-house service provider) which has been providing the services, that are to be outsourced, have deeply entrenched, informal, and ad hoc relationships with the users of the services. These relationships have been built up over a long period of time. Over this period, the internal service provider has provided a range of services - some of which are clearly identifiable, but others may be hidden, for example because specific services are provided to selected individuals such as the Managing Director or the Head of the Department. It is sometimes the case that no attempt has ever been made to define the services that the in-house service provider is providing. Those organisations without any formal service provision arrangements find it most difficult to define the scope of the services.

For other customers, it is easier to define the services or functions that should be outsourced. This would be the case, for example, where there are already internal arrangements which have all the features of a service provision arrangement. These organisations may be planning only to outsource these particular services or they may have in mind broadening the range of functions that are to be outsourced. Either way, some of the difficulty of defining services and service levels has already been gone through.

In addition to finding it difficult to define precisely what services are being provided and the levels at which these are to be provided, customers are often not sure which functions to outsource, because they are not sure what service providers can deliver and how much this will cost. If a customer is not sure what to outsource, one approach may be to include in the Request for Proposal (RFP) a wide range of functions that are capable of being outsourced and include a requirement in the documentation that the potential service provider provides separate pricing for these functions. For example, the customer may decide to approach the market place with a proposal to outsource all of its ICT functions which may include:

- The data centre
- Applications development
- Applications maintenance
- Desktop services
- Telecommunications
- Disaster recovery
- Training.

When a customer does not know which services to outsource, it frequently issues an RFP stating that it would only outsource those areas where it proves cost effective to do so. Potential service providers are asked to provide full details of how they would provide the range of services.

Just as important as defining the services that are to be outsourced, is defining the services that the customer wishes to keep in-house. This is an issue that should be given careful consideration: many of the benefits of outsourcing functions to an external service provider can be lost if the service providers task is made difficult because of important, lingering linkages to certain sections of the organisation which had close links with the previous in-house service provider. This all derives from the basic policy principle of why an organisation wants to outsource. What are the principal goals of outsourcing? Having these goals clearly in mind will simplify the 'what' question and facilitates the answer to the question what needs to be kept in-house. Sometimes it is difficult for an organisation that has been performing the services itself for a long period to surrender control of certain areas which it regards as important. However, if the organisation does not surrender control, many of the benefits that could arise from outsourcing may be lost.

How to Source Services

In addition to defining what functions to outsource, many customers have a difficult time determining which sites to include in the outsourcing arrangement. Customer's organisations can be spread across different geographic locations. The customers must decide if just one site is to be outsourced or if all the sites to be outsourced.

Another factor affecting this decision is the customer's management structure. If a customer has a decentralised structure, it is often difficult to reach a consensus about which site should be outsourced. The managers often have conflicting ideas about whether or not outsourcing is the right solution for all sites. This is usually less of a factor in public sector agencies where the decision to outsource is often made as a result of a centralised policy decision.

Issues to be considered when defining the scope of the services to be outsourced:
Whether or not:
- The customer currently provides services to other entities and if these services are to be included in the scope.
- The end users of the services have been established (employees, customers, suppliers, independent consultants).
- There are any existing outsourcing/subcontracting arrangements in place that cover the services to be outsourced.
  - If so, what are the costs associated with terminating or transferring these relationships.
- Assets will be sold or leased to the service provider.
- The customer has imposed a condition that their current employees are to be transferred to the successful service provider.
- There are any alternative structures that should be considered for the purposes of providing the services - such as forming a joint venture with the service provider or creating a separate legal entity out of the area to be outsourced and then selling that entity to the service provider.

It is also important for any customer wishing to outsource to have a strong understanding of the tasks performed by the staff currently responsible for the functions to be outsourced. It is important to address these issues early in the transaction for a number of reasons:

- If the customer does not know what services its staff provides it is difficult to define the services the customer wants the service provider to provide.
- If the information that is provided to it is not comprehensive and accurate, it is extremely difficult for the service provider to respond with useful, accurate information in relation to the services and costing.
- If the customer does not have a clear and comprehensive understanding of its current tasks, the customer is in a vulnerable position when it enters into negotiations with the service provider. The customer may find itself on the back foot during negotiations and unable to negotiate a cost effective deal.

Another area that is often overlooked until too late is the identification of those services that are regarded as 'critical'. It is crucial that these services be identified early in the SA development. If the customer has an understanding of its critical functions, it can negotiate higher standards and of course more stringent remedies if these critical functions are not met.

Factors Influencing the Service Specification

The most important part of every SA is the description of the services to be provided by the service provider. It is most important that the customer prepare this list itself because it is in the best position to be able to do this. It is also important that when the SA is signed, it contains a comprehensive list of these services. If it is discovered after the SA is signed that other services (which were already provided, but not listed in the SA) need to be provided, the service provider will understandably wish to charge an additional amount for the provision of these services.

The services being outsourced also need to be defined fully in which case the customer can be sure that it has brought to the attention of the service provider the services that it requires. The service provider can not be expected to know that the customer wishes a service to be provided, if the service is not described in the SA.

As part of the effort to describe the services to the greatest and most accurate extent possible, a number of customers hire a consultant familiar with outsourcing transactions to develop a comprehensive list of the services and the service levels historically provided by the in-house service provider. Customers are often reluctant to hire a consultant to perform this task because they think that they should be able to do it themselves - since they have been providing the services themselves for a considerable period. It is counter-productive to allow feelings of embarrassment or inadequacy to intrude in what is an absolutely critical task. It is often the quickest and most effective way to have such a list prepared - particularly if the in-house service provider is disenchanted that the services they provide are to be outsourced.

It is important to manage customer's expectations in respect of the abilities of the service provider. Do not start with what the service provider think people's expectations are or should be; start by asking people what are their expectations? Often the expectations are higher than what is reasonable.

Before an outsourcing relationship begins, stakeholders need to be aware of changes that need to take place before the services can be provided. It would be useful for both parties to have a clear understanding of the assets that the customer owns and if there is any thought that the service provider is going to purchase these. Even if the service provider is not going to purchase any equipment but is required to maintain these, upgrade them or replace them, it is extremely important that a comprehensive and accurate list of assets be prepared.

4.3.6 Service Levels

An issue that needs to be considered early in the SA development is service levels. Issues that need to be decided in relation to service levels are: the current level of service; the intended level of service; the measurement of the services; and the existence of industry standards for the services.

Service levels are an important aspect of the SA. Yet very often little attention is paid to these until very late in the transaction. Many of the same issues arise in defining service levels as arise in defining the scope of the services to be outsourced. For example, the in-house service providers have no expertise in preparing service level information and are reluctant to start doing this now because of they see no reason why the services should be outsourced. In order to ensure success in SA engagements, the Development Team must use a structured methodology to define service levels that is effective in achieving business objectives and driving the desired behaviours from external service providers.

Service providers are often willing to commit to providing service levels that the customer is currently providing. But if the customer is not certain what service levels it is currently providing, not only is it difficult for the service provider to provide accurate costing, it is not technically possible for the service provider to agree to meet the level of services currently being provided.

If service levels are not determined from the beginning it is possible to start implementation with a 'proof of concept' period in which service level performance is carefully measured against proposed or desired service levels. Prerequisite to do so is that specific and measurable levels are chosen from the very start of service delivery. During this phase parties normally agree not to apply financial penalties for not meeting levels.

The more information the customer has about its existing service levels the better the service levels it will be able to negotiate, and the easier it will be to monitor the service provider's performance after the SA has been signed.

If the customer is having difficulty preparing comprehensive and accurate service levels, it is advisable to seek expert assistance as soon as possible. Without detailed service levels and performance standards, it is impossible to measure the service provider's performance or effectively manage the service provider. Service levels are significant because they are often tied to a rebate provisions or a liquidated damages clause which requires the service provider to pay damages, issue credits or forego certain payments, if it fails to meet the specified service levels.

The majority of the Service Levels in an SA need to be measurable, using meaningful metrics. For the SLAs that are not measurable, both parties must be very careful with the description that is used to qualify the level of service expected. Many SAs, like many other Service Contracts, often provide that the customer or the service provider must use its 'best efforts' or 'reasonable efforts' in taking certain actions and preventing certain occurrences under the SA. The precise meaning of 'best efforts' is elusive. While the courts have generally recognised such obligations as substantial and legally enforceable, finding a generalised meaning for the term 'best efforts' has proved difficult. The courts have consistently held that the term 'best efforts' is vague and is subject to an analysis of all the surrounding circumstances. A party charged with an obligation to use its 'best efforts' must perform to the extent of his or her total capabilities. Just what this standard entails depends on the particular case and the agreement involved.

In relation to defining 'reasonable efforts', the courts have been equally ambiguous. It appears that the courts have concluded that this standard is no higher when the obligation is explicit than when the obligation has been omitted. The courts have stated that every contract contains an implied covenant that the parties will act in good faith and that their dealings will be fair.

If the courts have difficulty deciding what 'best efforts' and 'reasonable efforts' mean, how much more difficultly will the customer and the service provider have in agreeing on what this standard means. In all circumstances, it is far preferable to state in the SA that the service provider will provide the services at the levels specified in the SA, and the SA should specify precisely what those levels are. Frequently an ICT metric is not a true reflection of the value of a service provision as it does not address the impact to the business of good or bad service. In that way, the customer knows what to expect and the service provider knows what to provide. The service provider also knows how to cost the services and is less likely to raise the service charges as soon as the SA is signed.

When the negotiation team specifies actual metrics for the SLAs, they should adopt a customer perspective, that is, they should take an end-to-end view and not a component-by-component perspective. For example, separate metrics should not be specified for the network (or even worse, network components), servers and application(s). If such metrics are used it will appear as if an attempt is being made to conceal the actual results and credibility will be lost.

4.3.7   Non-Compliance

Non-Performance
As mentioned before, SAs which include SLAs are usually inherently more complex and wide-ranging than simpler service contracts. In outsourcing situations, these arrangements usually involve not only the provision of services but often the sale of the customer's assets and the elimination of a large number of positions from within the customer's organisation. Because of this, customers are in a very vulnerable position when the service provider does not provide the services at the agreed level. For this reason, it is wise to include various measures in the SA that can be implemented in an escalating fashion when the service provider does not meet its obligation.

For obvious reasons, it may be extremely difficult to terminate the SA immediately and attempt either to provide the services in-house or take on a new service provider. One of the easiest ways to ensure that the service provider meets its obligations is to put in place management arrangements which entail regular reviews of the service provider's performance. Initially regular monthly reviews are recommended which can be altered to quarterly or even biannually reviews. These arrangements should also ensure that the users are regularly surveyed to ensure that the SLA accurately reflects what the users wants, and that the users are in fact getting the service that they require.

Detecting Non-Performance
It may be that the SA, especially the SLA part of the SA, does not actually provide precise details of the levels of service that the customer requires. While this should have been done before the SA was signed, it is better to discover the inadequacies of the SA early on in the relationship than later on. Unfortunately, however, if the customer attempts

to introduce new services or new service levels into the SA after the SA is signed, it will almost certainly result in additional charges from the service provider. Obviously it is preferable that all these details are settled before the SA is signed.

The outsourcing agreement will proceed smoothly if the SA specifies precisely the services that the customer is to receive, and at what level. It is obviously in everybody's interest to ensure that obligations are properly met by both parties and that any tendency towards non-performance is picked up at an early stage and eliminated.

Customers are very quick to suggest the service provider is at fault, if there are any problems about non-performance. However, it is often the case that it is directly or indirectly the customer's fault that the service provider is not meeting its obligations. For example, the customer may have had an obligation to provide certain information, or to carry out certain tasks, or to provide certain equipment. Instead of suggesting that the service provider is at fault and moving to invoke remedies for non-performance, it is essential that the customers ensure that they are meeting all of their obligations and not hindering the service provider in the performance of its obligations.

Several of the SLAs contained in the SA should stipulate the use of reports to track and manage SLA compliance. Often, these reports are generated and provided for the customer by the service provider. Any SA that contains SLAs that require the use of reports to aid in management should also specify the details of the reports. At a minimum, details should specify the frequency of the report, content, method generated, method of delivery (or availability if web-based), frequency of reporting and availability for customer review. This type of arrangement keeps both parties honest. The major benefits of reporting are that the customer sees if the service provider is delivering the appropriate service and the service provider may use performance reports to alert the customer to other potential problems that may be unrelated to the service provider.

Resolution for Non-Performance

Once the customer has established that it is in fact the service provider who is at fault, it is important to have management and escalation arrangements in place which ensure that the non-performance issue can be dealt with quickly, effectively and in a manner that will not damage the delicate relationship between the parties. In an SA of any size, it is important to ensure that a committee is established at the identification of a non-compliance issue. This committee should comprise key personnel from the service provider's organisation and key personnel from the customer's organisation that can regularly consider any issues that arise. This committee could meet weekly, fortnightly or monthly.

While a formal meeting may be appropriate on a monthly basis, there should be more informal meetings on a regularly basis if there are critical services that are being provided. If an issue of non-performance does arise this should be initially discussed at the lowest management level to see if the issue can be resolved. If the issues cannot be resolved, then the matter should be immediately escalated to the committee for review. The committee should consider the issue in detail, assess whether there have been past issues of non-performance, how long the non-performance has been continuing, how serious the non-performance is et cetera. Hopefully the service provider will realise the seriousness of the situation and take steps immediately to remedy or eliminate the non-performance. If the non-performance continues, then the contractual remedies need to be invoked.

The contractual remedies for non-performance should also be invoked in an escalating manner. There are two commonly used remedies for non-performance. These remedies are variations on the same theme.

1. One of the remedies for non-performance is **liquidated damages**. Liquidated damages are an agreed on monetary remedy which is to be paid to the customer in the event of a specified breach by the service provider. The amount of liquidated damages must be a genuine pre-estimate of the damage that the customer is likely to incur if a specified breach occurs. Customers often have great difficulty trying to assess what this amount should be, and many customers abandon this as a remedy because of this difficulty.

   It is, however, a useful remedy and one that is both effective in the short-term and may stave off termination which is both damaging and disruptive to both parties. It is important, however, that the amount agreed as liquidated damages should be a genuine pre-estimate. If the amount is too high, the courts will refuse to enforce the provision because they would deem it to be a penalty. The customer would then be forced to take legal action for breach of the contract in the normal course of events - which is both time consuming and costly. If the amount of liquidated damages if far below the amount that the customer is likely to suffer if there is the specified breach, then the customer will not be receiving fair compensation for those breaches, and it is not therefore in the customer's interests to fix this figure too low.

2. **Rebate clauses** are clauses that take the form of adjustments to the base fee under the SA. For example, if the service provider fails to perform according to the service levels for a specified period of time, the rebate to the customer might take the form of a credit against the next month's base fee (or a reduction in the amount that is payable to the service provider). A provision of this nature is likely to be viewed as a liquidated damages clause by a court. Thus, if the provision fixes an unreasonably large amount to be foregone by the service provider, it may be regarded as a penalty.

The unreasonableness of a liquidated damages provision is judged at the time the SA was entered into as opposed to the time at which the damage arose. Although service providers typically resist including a liquidated damages clause in the SA, a persistent customer can get the service provider to accept such a clause, if the amount that is proposed is reasonable and a cap is placed on the amount of such damages payable.

It is important for a customer to realise that an enforceable liquidated damages provision precludes the customer from claiming actual damages for the specified breach. A customer cannot have both liquidated damages and actual damages, since the intent of the liquidated damages provision is to fix the amount of damages in instances where the precise damages are difficult to prove, or the parties wish to avoid protracted litigation.

Termination
The ultimate remedy for non-performance is the termination of the SA. All SAs should provide a means by which either party may terminate the SA on the occurrence of certain events. Most termination clauses in an SA provide specified grounds for termination by the customer.

The seven most common grounds for termination of an SA:
1. If the service provider has failed to provide the service at the agreed service level for a significant period of time, three months for example.
2. If the service provider has breached the customer's confidential information in a serious manner.
3. If the service provider assigns its rights otherwise than in accordance with the SA.
4. If the service provider becomes subject to any form of insolvency administration.
5. If there is a change in the ownership of the customer which, in the customer's view, will adversely affect the provision of the services.
6. If the service provider has committed a 'material' breach of the agreement to the extent that the customer, acting reasonably, considers it inappropriate that the SA continues.
7. If the customer is in breach of its obligation to pay the service fees for a defined period of time, three months for example.

There is often a tendency to include in an SA a provision whereby the customer may terminate where there is a 'serious breach' or a 'material breach' of the agreement. There is usually very little agreement between the parties during development of the SA about what these expressions actually mean. What is 'material' or 'serious' to one party may be not 'serious' or 'material' to the other party. All that these expressions do is create further antagonism and uncertainty and make it more difficult to resolve the situation.

If one party insists on using the expression 'material' or 'serious' then it is advisable for the other party to ask for a definition of what that party means by those expressions. If the party is not able to provide an explanation about what they mean, then it is advisable not to proceed with the use of these expressions. If the party is able to provide a clear explanation of what they mean by a 'serious' or 'material' breach, then these grounds should go into the termination clause as explicit grounds for termination.

Another common ground for termination of an SA is if the breaching party has failed to perform any of its obligations under the agreement, which breach has not been remedied by the breaching party after notice has been provided by the injured party. The injured party would normally give the breaching party a certain period to remedy the breach (such as 30 days, 60 days and 90 days). If this breach has not been remedied by the expiration of this period, the injured party may terminate the agreement.

When establishing the remedy period, the customer should consider how long it can realistically wait for the service provider to remedy the breach. In some cases, a 24 hour period during which services are not provided will cripple a customer's business. As a result, it is often necessary to establish different periods for different breaches.

An issue highlighted in recent years by terrorism is the need to rethink the purpose of force majeure provisions. Force majeure provisions can be combined and coordinated with disaster recovery and business continuation provisions. Disaster recovery and business continuity plans are meant to operate when certain force majeure events occur. The force majeure provision should not operate to relieve the service provider of the obligation to perform. While force majeure events might reduce the obligations of the service provider, they should not eliminate them. Instead, the contact should require the service provider do be part of the disaster recovery and business continuation process. In essence, the contract should specify the acts the service provider is to take in the event of particular force majeure events instead of simply excusing service provider performance.

As part of the termination, there should be clauses dealing with the cooperation of the current service provider in order to get the new service provider up and running in case of exercising the grounds for termination. Things to consider include procedures, tools and checks. This will normally happen in a case of breach of agreement and in that case the customer has to legally bind the 'old' provider to support the hand-over and to continue the delivery of service until the hand-over has been completed.

4.3.8 Flexibility

SAs are rarely for a term of less than three years and often extend for up to 10 years. Over such a period of time, the needs of the customer's business change.

Given the inevitability of change, it is important for flexibility to be built into an SA. The consequences for certain organisations of not having built flexibility into their SAs are becoming more evident. One of the characteristics of the so-called 'second wave of outsourcing' is the renegotiation of SAs because the SLAs which were originally agreed, say three or five years ago, no longer match the organisation's business requirements.

Frequently in ICT outsourcing transactions, the service provider charges the customer on the basis of service volumes. For example, the customer can agree to pay the service provider on a per transaction basis. This allows for a certain amount of change in the requirements of the customer without the need to amend the SA. This would be done on a long term contract, if the parties envisaged that volumes of card transactions, and volumes of ticket sales, could vary significantly.

Customers should consider whether or not to build into their SAs a capacity either to increase the scope of the services being provided by the service provider, or to decrease the scope.

An SA could increase in scope as follows:
- On day one, the service provider takes over the desktop functions.
- If the service provider performs satisfactorily in relation to the SLAs for desktop functions, the customer brings into scope the provision of help desk functions.
- If the service provider performs satisfactorily against the SLAs for help desk functions, then corporate applications support is brought into scope.
- Finally, network support is brought into scope, if the service provider meets all SLAs.

Conversely, the customer seeks to include in the SA a right to drop particular service functions out of scope in the event of continual sub-standard performance against SLAs.

Changes in technology may lead the customer to require new types of services, and render current services obsolete. Usually, the parties include in their agreement a mechanism to accommodate such change, for example, a 'change control' clause.

Unless the service level agreement can accommodate changes in technology, the customer who enters into a long-term outsourcing arrangement risks being locked into paying for a range of services that may become obsolete.

Some SAs are intended to compel the service provider to utilise the most up-to-date technology in the provision of the services.

Another specific variable which the parties should consider is the likelihood of change in the cost of living or change in salaries for ICT professionals. Such changes impact upon the rates which the service provider pays for the personnel it engages to provide the service. It is in the service provider's interests to ensure that the SA ties fees or prices to changes in an index, which reflects inflation, for example, the Consumer Price Index (CPI). Over a three, five or ten year term, this could be significant.

Whilst adjustments to reflect changes in CPI usually benefit the service provider, other adjustments might benefit the customer. If the cost of ICT resources are declining or if the parties expect that efficiencies in service delivery over time will enable the service provider to reduce its costs, 'open book' pricing will generally benefit the customer. This open book pricing allows the service provider to charge for its services a fee which represents a specific, pre-agreed margin on its actual cost of providing the services. Such open book pricing arrangements necessitate the inclusion of a mechanism in the SA which enables the customer to verify the service provider's costs. Verification might take place by way of periodic audit by the customer and its consultants, such as auditors retained by the customer.

A further layer of sophistication in such pricing arrangements is to include terms to the effect that the service provider's fees must remain at a specific percentage below the equivalent standard industry fees. This obviously raises the difficult issue of identifying a benchmark which represents the industry standard for such fees.

Those who are in the process of outsourcing must accommodate business change by layering the pricing in SAs, and by avoiding aggregated or lump sum pricing structures. Layered pricing refers to pricing which is broken down and allocated to the various specific elements of the service which is to be provided. Thus, change in one element can be accommodated more easily, without necessarily requiring renegotiation of all pricing.

Assuming that the participants have recognised that change is inevitable and built flexibility into their SAs, change must be managed.

The SA has the important function of documenting certain agreed expectations, and obligations, of the parties. It is critical that the SA documentation remain current with changes the parties may implement in the course of their relationship. Unless the underlying contractual documentation is correct, the parties have no certainty as to their rights and obligations, and their relationship at large.

SA participants must provide scope for implementing changes to SAs. Under such procedures, changes required by a party must be documented, and submitted for assessment by the other party. Only following assessment and full consideration by the parties of the impact of the change on such things as fees and timeframes, does the change get implemented? Once the parties have agreed on the change, the formal contractual documentation is amended.

4.4 The Service Level Agreement Specification

The specification phase comprises the following four steps:
1. Define
2. Monitor and Agree
3. Document
4. Review and Optimise.

This sequence is repeated for each and every Service Level Agreement (SLA). An individual SLA can repeat the sequence as many times as necessary.

4.4.1 Define
The first step is to define an SLA. It is better to have several SLAs based on shared critical service provisions than an SLA for every service provision.

This should be done in consultation with representatives from all identified parties that use, supply or rely on the service. This includes current and intended suppliers of the service if they are different.

4.4.2 Monitor and Agree
It is unusual that any metrics will be available at the onset of the negotiations. The service provider needs to begin monitoring the initially identified services as soon as possible. This provides a current level of service base line to use. This step involves the DT and other involved parties monitoring the current provision of the service, and agreeing on all the aspects of the specification of the service.

4.4.3 Document

The next step is to document clearly and in line with previously agreed upon standards, all aspects of the service. This needs to done in relatively simple language, as not everybody that needs to use the document in the future will be technically, legally or financially proficient.

4.4.4 Review and Optimise

Finally, the documented SLA should be submitted to a review board. This board comprises of at least one representative from each discernable group that has a stake in the services and their provision. This is different from the Development Team as can be seen in Table 4.

Development Team	Review Board
Sales Representative	Service Provider
Technical	Customer
Legal Advisor	User Group 1
Financial Advisor	User Group 2
Customer	User Group n
	Service Manager
	Service Team
	Financial Manager
	Legal Manager

Table 4 *The Review Board*

The board has the responsibility to ensure that all interests are taken into account and that the newly-documented SLA can be understood to mean exactly what was agreed upon in step two. The DT should then optimise the SLA documentation inline with the review board's suggestions, or send the SLA through another iteration of these steps.

4.5 Sign-off and Promotion

Once the DT has successfully documented all the agreed service levels, and included all additional legal and financial clauses, the major stakeholders need to sign off on the final document. This final document should have also resulted in a healthy trusting relationship between all the stakeholders. It must be remembered that the more executives that sign off on the agreement, the more weight it will carry with all stakeholders.

The DT must then promote the existence of the SA to everybody it effects. This can be done by simple informative emails or on group notice boards. The help desks and service agents must be educated on the agreement and the ramifications of it.

The DT then hands over the management of the agreement and business relationship to the Service Management department. This involves a live SA that needs continuous service management in order to maintain customer satisfaction, business alignment, process improvement and implementing cost-quality weighs (better services, more or less options, adjusted pricing, accumulation of new organisation needs / changes infrastructure et cetera).

The link between the two phases provides for continual service improvements. Further, this link provides the organisation with the facility to continually assess their ability to provide managed services.

4.6   Conclusion

Strong business relationships are a key component of a sustainable partnership. The successful development of an SA is vital to the continuing relationship between a customer and a service provider. An SA is supposed to document the terms of the business relationship. This chapter detailed a model for the development of these critical documents. Emphasis has been placed on all the relevant components, forces and processes that combine to produce a Service Agreement that will provide the necessary foundation for a successful business partnership.

CHAPTER 5

Conclusion

The true value of ICT service provision can only be realised when the services it provides are solutions to identified business needs that are both practical and reliable. In order to achieve this, these services need to be well managed. This improvement in the provision and management of services promotes the credibility of the industry while improving customer loyalty and satisfaction. Improvement will ultimately combine to allow the ICT industry to mature and regain much of the ground lost in the late 1990's and early 2000's.

Service providers must ensure their capacity to provide and manage identified services. This introspection is best performed in an environment that does not contain a customer.

Fundamental to SM, and its subsequent implementation, is the collaboration between customer and provider. This collaboration between these parties begins when service expectations are set and then develops into a relationship when these service requirements are being satisfied. This relationship evolves further as each party is committed to refining the business agreement. The future of successful SM lies in the recognition of the importance of a communicative relationship between customer and provider. Successful SM is possible when providers, who are confident of their ability to manage levels of service, and customers who are aware of their service requirements, enter into such a communicative relationship.

In order to develop a business relationship based on a managed services environment, the implementation and management of these services needs to be structured and formalised. This book presents a comprehensive analysis of SM and a framework for the implementation thereof. This framework also provides for the development of Service Catalogues. Service Agreements are a key component of SM. This book recognises this and presents a model for their negotiation and development.

CHAPTER 6

Bibliography

Abeck, S., D. Boning, & A. Koppel, (1999). *How to Support the Negotiation of Service Level Agreements for your Client/Server Application.* Germany: Institute for Telematics, University of Karlsruhe. Joint Meeting of the Third World Multiconference on Systemics, Cybernetics and Informatics (SCI'99) and the Fifth International Conference on Information Systems Analysis and Synthesis (ISAS'99).

Albaugh, V. & H. Madduri (2004). The Utility Metering Service of the Universal Management Infrastructure. In *IBM Systems Journal.* Vol. 43, No. 1, 2004 (pp179-189).

Allen, D. (2002). Quest Introduces On- and Off-Net SLAs. In: *Network Magazine.* (p14)

Allen, J., D. Gabbard & C. May (2003). *Content Guidance for an MSS Service Level Agreement.* Carnegie Mellon Software Engineering Institute.

Aman, J., C. Eilert, D. Emmes, P. Yocom & D. Dillenberger (1997). Adaptive Algorithms for Managing a Distributed Data Processing Workload. In *IBM Systems Journal, 36(2)*, 242–283.

Appleby, K., J. Breh, G. Breiter, H. Daur, T. Eilam, S.A. Fakhouri, G. Hunt, T. Lu, S. Miller, L. Mummert, J. Pershing & H. Wagner (2004). Using a Utility Computing Framework to Develop Utility Systems. In *IBM Systems Journal.* Vol. 43 No. 1, 2004 (pp97-120).

Appleby, K., S. Fakhouri, L. Fong, G. Goldszmidt, M. Kalantar, S. Krishnakumar, D.P. Pasel, J. Pershing & B. Rochwerger (2001). *Océano – SLA Based Management of a Computing Utility.* IBM TJ Watson Research Center.

Arabas, P., M. Kamola, K. Malinowski, & M. Malowidzki (2002). *Pricing for IP Networks and Services.* Warsaw (Poland): Warsaw University of Technology, Institute of Control and Computation Engineering.

Axios Systems (2002). *An Introduction to IT Service Management Best Practice.* Axios Systems Limited Whitepaper. Axios Systems Limited.

Axios Systems (2003). *Taking You Beyond ITIL.* BS15000 Whitepaper 2. Axios Systems Limited.

Axios Systems (2004). *Everybody's doing ITIL - or are they?* Axios Systems Limited BS15000 Whitepaper. Axios Systems Limited.

Babinec, T. & C. Mehta (1998). *Thinking About Exact Statistics.* service providerSS Software.

Becta (2004). Service Level Management. Coventry: British Educational Communications and Technology Agency.

Behling, J. (2003). *Accenture Back to Basics.* Accenture Publications.

Blum, R. (2002) *Service Level Management and Service Level Agreements.* International Network Services. 25 March 2002.

Boardman, B. (2001). Network and Systems Management. In *Network Computing 17,* December 2001.

Boshoff, T. (2005). The Pitfalls of ITIL. In *Computing SA, 18 April 2005.*

Bouillet, E, D. Mitra & K. Ramakrishnan (2002). The Structure and Management of Service Level Agreements in Networks. In *IEEE Journal on Selected Areas in Communications* Vol. 20, No. 4, May 2002.

Bouman, J., Trienekens & M. van der Zwan (1999). *Specification of Service Level Agreements, Clarifying Concepts on the Basis of Practical Research.* Improve Quality Services. www.improveqs.nl/pdf/sla.pdf

Brittain, K. & R. Matlus (2002). *Road Map for IT Service-Level Management.* Gartner Research 28 January 2002.

Brittain, K. (2002). *Infrastructure Management: Standards, Best Practices, ITIL.* Gartner Research 10 June 2002.

Bryant, S. (2002). *Blueprint for an Exchange Service Level Agreement.* MsExchange. http://www.msexchange.org/tutorials/Blueprint_for_an_Exchange_Service_ Level_Agreement.html.

Buco, M., R. Chang, L. Luan, C. Ward, J. Wolf, & P. Yu (2004). Utility Computing SLA Management based on business objectives. IBM Systems Journal, Vol. 43 No. 1 2004 (pp159-178).

Caine, A. (1997). *Negotiating An Effective Service Level Agreement.* Gilbert and Tobin Lawyers. http://www.gtlaw.com.au/gt/site/articleIDs/B685FA264603E965CA 256D1E000CF754?open&&ui=dom&template=domGTPrint.

Crawford, C., & A. Dan (2002). Addressing the Need for a Flexible Modelling Framework in Autonomic Computing. In *IEEE/ACM International Symposium on Modelling, Analysis and Simulation of Computer and Telecommunications Systems* (MASCOTS 2002).

Cronk, T., J. Gorball, L. Wiener, J. Brooks, M. Fernandez, W. Lambert, B. Gross & R. Laverty (2002). *SLA Navigator.* The Computing Technology Industry Association.

Dan, A., H. Ludwig & G. Pacifici (2003). *Web Services Differentiation with Service Level Agreements.* IBM Developer Works. http://citeseer.ist.psu.edu/697275.html.

Deckelman, B. (1997). *Negotiating Effective SLAs.* Outsourcing Center. http://www.outsourcing-sla.com/negotiating.html.

Drake, J. (2000). *The HP IT Service Management Reference Model.* Hewlett-Packard Company.

Drogseth, A. (2001). *Stepping up to Multi-tiered service level agreements.* Network World Fusion. http://www.nwfusion.com/newsletters/nsm/2001/00863051.html.

Empirix (2003). *Managing Service Level Agreements with C.A.R.E.* Empirix.

Engel, F. (2002). The Role of Service Level Agreements in the Internet Service Provider Industry. In *International Journal of Network Management*. 9, (pp299-301).

Enterprise Management Associates (2002). *Implementing SLAs: Tools for Success*. Compuware Corporation.

Erickson-Harris, L. (2003). Help with SLM. *Network World Fusion*, 21 July 2003.

Erikson-Harris, L. (2003). Six Sigma and ITIL: Two methods of Managing Services. In *Network World 04/14/03*. http://www.networkworld.com/newsletters/nsm/2003/0414nsm1.html.

Figg, J. (2000). Outsourcing - A Runaway Train. Internal Auditor, June 2000 (pp49-55).

Fluke Networks (2004). *Improve Networked Application Performance through SLAs*. Fluke Networks. http://www.flukenetworks.com.

Gardner, D. (2000). How do we Start a Project? Ensuring the Right Sponsorship, Stakeholder Alignment and Thoughtful Preparation for a Project. In *Proceedings of the Project Management Institute Annual Seminars and Symposium*. September 2000, Houston Texas.

Gillet-Liloia, T. & J. Kotwica (2002). *Executives guide to Service Level Agreements*. Darwin Executive Guides.

Gomolski, B. (2004). It's Time to Re-engineer IT. *In Computerworld, 38(16)*, April 19 2004.

Gray, J. (2000). *Negotiating An Effective Service Level Agreement II*. Gilbert and Tobin Lawyers. http://www.gtlaw.com.au/gt/site/articleIDs/4315E4487A98C1B9CA256D32001BAD38?open&&ui=dom&template=domGTPrint.

Grubic, J. & D. Thomson (2002). Negotiating a Superior Logistics Services Agreement. In *Logistics Quarterly Vol.8, Issue 2 – Article 1*.

Hanneman, A., M. Sailer & D. Schmitz (2004). Assured Service Quality by Improved Fault Management. In *Proceedings of the 2nd international conference on Service Oriented Computing*. ACM Press. (pp173-182).

Hartley, K. (2005). Defining Effective Service Level Agreements for Network Operation and Maintenance. In *Bell Labs Technical Journal 9(4)*.

Hartman, F. & E. Romahn (1999). Trust: A New Tool for Project Managers. In *Proceedings of the 30th Annual Project Management Institute 1999 Seminars & Symposium*. Philadelphia, Pennsylvania, USA.

Hautamäki, J., T. Lahteenmäki & N. Rimpilä (2004). *An Assessment of Maturity Level of the IT Service Management*. Institute of Information Technology, Jyvaskyla Polytechnic.

Havenstein, H. (2003). CRM Crisis Aservice provider's Save the Day. At *InfoWorld.com*.

He, L. & J. Walrand (2004). *Dynamic Provisioning of Service Level Agreements between Interconnected Networks*. Dept of Electrical Engineering and Computer Science, University of California at Berkeley.

Hechenleitner, B. & D. Hetzer (2002). *Toolkit for Quality of Service and Resource Optimisation.* Salzburg, Austria: Salzburg University.

Heine, J. (2004). *Management Update: Improving Service-Level Agreements in Contracts.* Gartner Research.

Hiles, A. (1999). *The Complete IT Guide to Service Level Agreements – Matching Service Quality to Business Needs.* Rothstein Associates Inc: Brookfield, CT.

Hiles, A. (2002). *The Complete Guide to IT Service Level Agreements: Aligning IT Service to Business Needs.* Brookfield, CN: Rothstein Associates Inc.

Human Sciences Research Council (2003). *Human Resources Development Review.* HSRC South Africa.

Information Week (2002). Behind the Numbers. At *Informationweek.com.*

International Engineering Consortium. *Service-Level Management.* International Engineering Consortium.

InterPromUSA (2002). *Managing SLAs.* InterPromUSA.

Itworld (2001). 10 myths about service-level agreements. At *ITworld.com* 4/27/2001.

Janssen, M. & A. Jona (2004). Issues in Relationship Management for Obtaining the Benefits of a Shared Service Center. In *Proceedings of the 6th international conference on Electronic Commerce ICEC '04.* ACM Press.

Johnson, A. & J. Rollins (2004). *Improving Business Performance.* Accenture.

Karten, N. (1999). Establishing Service Level Agreements. At *Karten Website.*

Karten, N. (1999). Why Service Level Agreements Fail. At *Karten Website.*

Karten, N. (2004). With Service Agreements, Less is More. In *Information Systems Management,* Vol. 21, Issue 4.

Kay, R. (2002). QuickStudy: System Development Life Cycle. In Computerworld. 14 May 2002.

Keller, A. & L. Heiko (2002). Defining and Monitoring Service Level Agreements for Dynamic e-Business. At *16th System Administration Conference.* Philadelphia, PA, USA: The USENIX Association.

Kettinger, J. & C. Lee (1997). Pragmatic Perspectives on the Measurement of Information Systems Service Quality. In *MIS Quarterly June 1997.* Vol. 21 Issue 2, p223, 18p.

Koch, C. (1998). Put IT in Writing. In *CIO Magazine.* Nov. 15, 1998

Kuebler, D. & W. Eibach (2001). Metering and Accounting for Web Services. At *IBM Developer Works.*

LaBounty, C. (2004). *Implementing Service Level Management.* LaBounty Associates Publications.

Lacity, M. & R. Hirschheim (1995). *Information Systems Outsourcing.* Chichester, England: John Wiley & Sons Ltd.

Laughlin, K. (2004). Sending Out an SLA. In *America's Network,* Vol. 108, Issue 6.

Lawes, A. (2004). *About Best Practice.* itSMF.

Lehr, W. & L. McKnight (2002). Show Me The Money: Contracts and Agents in Service Level Agreement Markets. At *Program on Internet and Telecoms Convergence, MIT.*

Leon, M. (2001). Agreements on the Level. At *InfoWorld.com*

Leonard, A. (2002). A Conceptual Framework for Managing Relationships between participants During IT Service and Support Activities. In *SA Journal of Industrial Engineering, 2002 Volume 13, Issue 2.*

Leopoldi, R. (2002). *ITSM: A description of a Service Catalogue.* RL Consulting.

Leopoldi, R. (2002). *ITSM: A Description of Service Level Agreements.* RL Consulting.

Leopoldi, R. (2002). *ITSM: Service Management.* RL Consulting.

Levine, S. (2003). Service Management: Uncharted Territory. In *America's Network, 15* January 2003.

Lewis, L. & P. Ray (1999). Service Level Management. Definition, Architecture, and Research Challenges. In *Proceedings of Global Telecommunications Conference GLOBECOM'99 1999, 3 1974–1978.*

Lewis, L. (1999). *Service Level Management for Enterprise Networks.* Artech House, INC.

Liu, Z., S. Squillante & J. Wolf (2001). *On Maximising Service-Level-Agreement Profits.* IBM TJ Watson Research Center.

Logan, I. (2004). *Initiating the SLA Culture.* ITIL People.

Ludwig, H. (2004). *Web Services QoS: External SLAs and Internal Policies.* IBM TJ Watson Research Center.

Ludwig, H., A. Keller, A. Dan & R. King (2002). A Service Level Agreement Language for Dynamic Electronic Services. In *Proceedings of WECWIS 2002, Newport Beach, CA, USA,* pp. 25 - 32. Los Alamitos: IEEE Computer Society.

Matlus, R. & K. Brittain (2002). *Creating a Service Level Agreement for the IS Organisation.* Gartner Group.

Maurer, W., L. Scardino, & A. Young (2004). *Guidelines to Develop SLAs for Application Outsourcing Deals.* Gartner Research.

McKeen, J., H. Smith & S. Singh (2005). Developments in Practice XVI: A Framework for enhancing IT Capabilities. In *Communications of the Association for Information Systems,* Volume 15, 2005.

Microsoft (2003). *Managing the Windows Server Platform.* Microsoft.

Microsoft (2003). *Service Level Management.* Microsoft.

Mingay, S. & M. Govekar (2002). *ITIL's Service Level Management Strength is in its Integration.* Gartner Research.

Mingay, S. (2004). *How Managing Services Using ITIL Profited an IT Department.* Gartner Research Note. Gartner Research.

Morgan, C. & J. Yallof (2003). *Beyond Performance Standards.* Benefits Quarterly. Third Quarter 2003 (pp17-22).

Muller, N. (1999). Managing Service Level Agreements. In *International Journal of Network Management,* Volume 9 Issue 3 1999.

Musich, P. (2003). *Managing Services to a T.* Enterprise News and Reviews, EWeek, May 19 (p40).

Navarro, L. (2001). Information Security Risks and Managed Security Service. In *Information Security Technical Report,* Vol 6, No. 3.

Network Physics (2003). *Bridging the Network Management Gap.* Network Physics.

Network Physics (2003). *Go With the Flow.* Network Physics.

Network Physics (2004). *Flow Based Network Management.* Network Physics.

Pisello, T. (2003). The Marriage of ROI and SLA. In *Computerworld.* Vol. 37 Issue 42,p52.

Pras, A. & R. Sprenkels (2001). *Service Level Agreements.* The Internet Next Generation Project.

Proxima Technology (2003). *Six Sigma for IT Service Management.* White Paper prepared by Enterprise Management Associates.

Pugh, N. (2001). What Constitutes a good SLA? In *Communication News,* July 2001, (pp44-45).

Rappa, M. (2004). The Utility Business Model and the Future of Computing Services. In *IBM Systems Journal,* Vol. 43, No. 1, (pp32-42).

Rockart, J., M. Earl & J. Ross (1996). Eight Imperatives for the New IT Organisation. In *Sloan Management Review, 36(1) Fall.*

Ross Research (2004). F&A Outsourcing. In *Financial Executive March/April 2004* (p51-57)

Ross, J. & G. Westerman (2004). Preparing for Utility Computing. In *IBM Systems Journal.* www.research.ibm.com/journal/sj/431/ross.pdf.

Sabherwal, R. (1999). The role of Trust in Outsourced IS Development Projects. In *Communications of the ACM.* http://portal.acm.org/citation.cfm?id=293411.293485

Santana, J. (2004). Tips for Crafting Better Outsourcing Relationships. In *Tech Republic.* http://whitepapers.techrepublic.com.com/abstract.aspx?docid=172585&promo= 300111.

Sauer, C., L. Liu & K. Johnston (1999). Enterprise-Level Project Management Capabilities: A Comparison of the Construction and IT Services Industries. In *Proceeding of the 20th international conference on Information Systems.* Association for Information Systems.

Savvas, A. (2004). Organisations failing to use SLAs to manage system performance. In *Computer Weekly;* p23, 1/4p, 1 chart.

Schmidt, H. (2000). Service Level Agreements Based on Business Process Modelling. Munich, Germany: University of Munich.

Shih, G. & S. Shim (2002). A Service Management Framework for M-Commerce Applications. In *Mobile Networks and Applications, 7.* Kluwer Academic Publishers.

SM Thacker and Associates (2000). *Guide to Service Level Agreements.* SM Thacker and Associates.

Smit, K. (2004). *The Key to Quality Service Level Management.* ITIL People. http://www.itilpeople.com/articles/key%20to%20SLM.htm.

Smith, R. (1995). *Business Continuity Planning and Service Level Agreements.* Information Management and Computer Security.

Sturm, R. & L. Erickson-Harris (2003). *SLM Solutions: A Buyers Guide.* Enterprise Management Associates.

Sturm, R. (2000). The Truth About Service-Level Management. In *InformationWeek News,* 8 May 2000.

Sturm, R. (2001a). The Functions of Service-Level Management. In *Network World Fusion,* 17 September 2001.

Sturm, R. (2001b). Assessing Service Availability. At *Network World Fusion.*

Sturm, R. (2001c). Response time tools for SLM. At *Network World Fusion.*

Sturm, R. (2001d). Choosing SLM Tools. At *Network World Fusion.* October 8, 2001.

Sturm, R. (2001e). Who can you trust with your SLA? At *Network World Fusion.* November 28, 2001.

Sturm, R. (2001f). Real SLM Means Being Proactive. At *Network World Fusion.* December 3, 2001.

Sturm, R. (2002a). Look Beyond IT for Service-Level Management Successes. At *Network World Fusion,* 7 January 2002.

Sturm, R. (2002b). Reporting for SLM. At *Network World Fusion, 7 February 2002.*

Sturm, R. (2002c). Service-Level Management: What is in it for IT. At *Network World Fusion,* 10 April 2002.

Sturm, R. (2002d). Reporting for SLM. At *Nextslm.org.* February 2002

Sturm, R. (2002e). Be Reasonable with SLAs. At *Network World Fusion.* February 4, 2002.

Sturm, R. (2002f). Getting Ready for SLAs. At *Network World Fusion.* May 29, 2002.

Sturm, R. (2002g). Look Beyond IT for SLM Successes. At *Network World Fusion.* January 7, 2002.

Sturm, R. (2002h). Defining SLM Tools. At *Network World Fusion.* June 3, 2002.

Sturm, R. (2002i). Do Your Homework before writing SLAs. At *Network World Fusion.* July 3 2003.

Sturm, R. (2002j). Don't sign a SLA you cant meet. At *Network World Fusion.* June 17, 2002.

Sturm, R. (2002k). What do Users want from SLM? At *Network World Fusion.* March 27, 2002.

Sturm, R. (2002l). Service Level Management: The Big Picture. At *Slminfo.org.*

Sturm, R. (2004). *SLM Solutions: A Buyers Guide SE.* Enterprise Management Associates.

Sturm, R., W. Morris & M. Jander (2000). *Foundations of Service Level Management.* Indiana: Sams.

Syntel (2003). *How to Outsource.* Syntel.

Tanenbaum, W. (2004). Revisiting Key Provisions in Software and Outsourcing Agreements. In *Journal of Internet Law.* Volume 6, Number 9, March 2003, pages 1Â–7.

Terasa Settas (2004). *BS15000 Standard in IT Service Management.* Foster-Melliar.

Texas Telecommunications Infrastructure Fund Board (unknown). *The Service Level Agreement.* Texas Telecommunications Infrastructure Fund Board.

The International Engineering Consortium (2002). Client Care. In *The International Engineering Consortium.*

The IT Infrastructure Library (2003). *Service Delivery.* The Stationery Office.

The IT Infrastructure Library (2004a). *Service Support.* The Stationery Office.

The IT Infrastructure Library (2004b). *Planning to Implement Service Management.* The Stationery Office.

The ITIL & ITSM World (2005). *Service Level Management.* ITSM World. http://www.itil-itsm-world.com/itil-6.htm.

Verma, D. (1999). *Supporting Service Level Agreements on IP Networks.* Macmillan Technical Publishing.

Visual Networks, Inc. & Tellechoice (2002). *Carrier Service Level Agreements.* The International Engineering Consortium.

Walder, B. (1998). *Service Level Agreements.* The Network Security Services Group.

Walker, C. (1996). Client Service Level Agreements. Brisbane, Australia: Griffith University.

Ward, J. (2001). *How to Build a Service Catalogue.* Tech Republic. http://whitepapers.techrepublic.com.com/abstract.aspx?docid=172735&promo=300111.

Wustenhoff, E. (2002). *Service Level Agreement in the Data Center.* Sun Microsystems.

Wylder, B. (1998). *Service Level Agreements.* United Kingdom: NSS.

Yallof, J. & C. Morgan (2003). Beyond Performance Standards: How to Get the Most From Your Outsourcing Relationship. In *Benefits Quarterly, Third Quarter 2003* p. 17-22.

Yarnall, P. (2004). Focus on the Business. In *Computer Weekly, 15 June 2004.*